DESTINED

DESTINED

Brandi Burr MacCurdy

HL

First Printing: 2016

ISBN 978-1-329-94419-0

CHAPTER 1

Becca waited eagerly for her best friend, Emma Reece, to enter the classroom. Becca had taken a desk in the back of the French class and had parked her book bag on the top of the desk beside her; for Emma.

Rhythmically tapping her toes against the carpet, she imagined Emma's reaction to the difference in Becca's appearance. Last night she had decided to mark the beginning of the end of her Freshman year in high school with a new hair style. She had talked her mother into chopping off her dark brown waves into a chic bob and dying it blonde. Her mother was hesitant at first, worried about what her father would say when and if he ever made it home. But after some persuading, it was decided that Becca was free to do with her hair as she pleased.

Becca sat up when she saw Emma swing open the door and saunter in.

Emma had been Becca's best friend since fifth grade. She was much less outgoing than Becca but they meshed perfectly. Emma's black hair was French braided and centered down her back. When her unusual blue eyes met Becca's Emma's mouth dropped.

"No way!" Emma picked up her pace and stood in front of Becca, "it's fantastic!" She reached out and touched Becca's blonde locks that now hung just at her chin. Yesterday her hair had been nearly to her waist, "what did your mom say?"

Becca laughed with confirmation, "She didn't care too much. Told me afterward it was a change, but nice," she shook her head so her hair would move about, "Ben wasn't so sure about it. He freaked out a little."

Ben was Becca's two-year-old brother. A major change of appearance to someone he sees everyday would upset a toddler.

Emma nodded, "What did your dad say?" she asked, squinting her eyes.

Becca bit down on her bottom lip, shrugged and raised her left eyebrow, "Nothing. He hasn't come home yet to see it."

Mr. McKenon was more like a ghost than a father. Since Ben had been born he was on and off the road, taking truck driving jobs to make ends meet. Lydia, Becca's mother, worked as a sheriff's dispatcher. It was one of the only jobs she was able to find that provided child care in-building for Ben and allowed flexible hours to take and pick up Becca from school.

Smiling sympathetically, Emma took her seat, "I just love it!" she said again, handing Becca her book bag that had been saving her seat.

"Me, too," Becca laughed again and straightened in her seat. The classroom was filling up quickly. Today was the first day of new classes, the last quarter of school was beginning. Freshman year had gone by slowly. She felt if she had been fifteen for four years already, not just a few months.

"Hey," Emma's whisper was harsh, "hot guys, two o'clock," her face turned red as she pointed her head toward the front of the classroom.

Becca once again sat up in her seat and looked forward. Emma was definitely the shy one; Becca was quite the opposite of shy.

Walking into the French classroom were two boys. They each were holding their books and laughing loudly at something inaudible. One she recognized right away as a Junior, Paul Martin. He was tall and thin with black hair cut real short and a smile that took up most of his face. He was a forward on the basketball team and had sat beside her in Algebra last quarter. Not the smartest of guys, but nice. And handsome.

The other boy she hadn't seen before. She would have remembered him. The smile on his face was contagious and when he glanced at her as he sat in the desk directly in front of her, her heart fluttered.

Turning back to Emma, Becca grinned and rapidly raised her eyebrows. He was beautiful. He was far too friendly with Paul to be a new student she concluded. He had on a pair of khaki cargo shorts and a blue collared polo shirt. His blonde hair was cut and gelled evenly.

Paul sat down in the desk to Becca's right and after she finished silently giggling with Emma, she turned back to face the front of the room, and stare at the back of the mystery boys head.

"Becca?" Paul gasped noticing her.

BINGO, she thought to herself. She turned to Paul and smiled, "Hey, Paul. How are you?" she asked politely.

She took note that when she spoke, the boy in front of her had turned around also.

"Good," he said slowly, "you look different," he smiled, reaching out to playfully tug at her newly shortened hair, "it's nice," he nodded and leaned back to look around Becca, "hey Emma."

Emma gave a small wave. She had a crush on Paul since November, when in Fitness class he reached out and stopped a runaway basketball from creaming her in the back of the head. It was sweet.

"Thank you," Becca answered and swiveled slightly to face the gorgeous smiling boy in front of her, "hi, I'm Becca."

His smile was consistent, it didn't leave his face, "Jamie," he said with a slight nod.

"Are you new? I haven't seen you before," Becca asked, holding his gaze. She could hear Emma taking gasps beside her.

"Uh, no," Jamie said, "been here since the beginning. I'm a Junior. I've seen you before, I think," he squinted his eyes questioningly, "you used to have long, brown hair, right? You two are always together," he said motioning toward Emma and smiling at her.

"You've got it," Becca nodded.

"I've noticed you before," Jamie nodded also and laughed, "you're a Freshman, right?"

EXCELLENT, she sarcastically thought to herself. Emma's low groan resonated.

"I am," she gritted her teeth and shrugged, smiling sideways.

"Mr. Enders, Miss. McKenon, would it be alright with you to start class today?" Mrs. Camosal asked from the front of the room.

Jamie rolled his eyes hard before turning around in his seat, "We're sorry, Ma'am," Becca called out as she glided her textbook and notebook out of her bag.

French had been nonstop and left not one second of time for Jamie to turn back to face Becca again until the end of class. When the bell rang, Becca felt her stomach drop. She didn't want class to be over.

"Nice to meet you," Jamie said to her as they both gathered their books, "guess I'll see you tomorrow," he smiled at her as she pulled her bag on her shoulder.

His smiled made goosebumps rise on her skin. She nodded, "See you then," she smiled back, waved to Paul as he smirked and followed Jamie out the door.

"Becca! He's gorgeous!" Emma flew around the desks and clamped down on Becca's forearm, "he kept smiling at you, oh I bet he likes you." She said excitedly.

"He's a Junior, Em," Becca widened her eyes, "he's probably seventeen, I'm fifteen, he probably thinks I'm too young," she hated saying that. It made her feel like a child.

"Do you think Paul thinks I'm too young?" Emma asked, her head tilted, her thin lips frowning.

"Everyone is different. You seem older than me, Paul seems younger than you," Becca shrugged as they headed into the hallway and navigated their way into the English wing. Again they had the same class, again they sat next to each other. But no Jamie in this class.

Becca's best subject was English. She loved writing, she loved grammar. And it took her little effort to excel in the subject.

While Mrs. Stegall explained the course and the required reading, Becca let her mind rest on Jamie. Being two years apart, they probably would only have French class together, so there was a good chance that would be the only time she'd see him. Unless she managed to glimpse him in the hallways. Quickly she scanned through her classes; French, English, Accounting and Biology. He could perhaps be in her Accounting class and in the science wing depending on his schedule. Accounting was the only class Becca didn't have with Emma.

Before she realized it, the dismissal bell had rung, causing her to jump in her seat. She'd spent nearly an hour concocting a plan to see Jamie as much as possible. She definitely was smitten with Jamie Enders. Her heart raced about as quickly as her eyes had scanned the halls while she and Emma walked to their next class.

"Crushing already?" Emma asked, being over observant.

"Like you wouldn't believe," Becca admitted, "wish age wasn't a thing."

"You're thinking about it too much. It's not like he's fifty years older than you," Emma smirked, "it's probably not that big of a deal to anyone. Besides, love knows no bounds," she said dramatically.

Becca was still giggling when they parted and headed into their respective classes. The room where the Accounting course was being held had long tables instead of individual desks, with four chairs at each. There were three seats already taken in the room. She made a dash to the last table, last seat against the wall. She liked being able to overlook the entire class and be out of the direct eye line of any teacher. She was a good student, but was also easily distracted. She had been shamefully caught on more than one occasion staring off into empty space and daydreaming. Being in the back of the room ran less risk of getting caught.

Pulling out her notebook and a pen, she stacked them on her table top and leaned forward. Resting her elbows on the top, her chin on her palms.

She felt her stomach twitch when Jamie crossed the threshold of the classroom. How could she be so lucky? She sat up and uncharacteristically become nervous, staring down at her notebook. Feverishly she wanted to run out and tell Emma, but the bell would ring at any second.

"Hey!"

She looked up, somehow knowing he was talking to her.

"Guess I won't have to wait until tomorrow to see you," he said smiling at her, of course, but with a twinge of red in his cheeks.

His comment made her skin feel hot.

"Saving this for anyone?" He pointed at the chair next to her.

"Nope, it's all yours. Emma has Computer Tech," she over explained and instantly felt ridiculous.

He nodded as he sat down, placing his books beside hers, "So does Paul. He'll be happy," his smile turned slightly wicked.

Becca snapped out of her own elation for a moment and did a double take, "What do you mean he'll be happy?" she asked, leaning into him.

Jamie's smile went crooked and he shrugged, "Paul likes Emma, but he's afraid he'll scare her. Guess she's really shy," he shrugged again and Becca noticed that his blue eyes were breathtaking.

Now she really wanted to sprint across the hall, "Oh, he won't scare her," she shook her head, "she may have a heart attack but it would be from shock. She likes him too, but," she paused and decided to go with her comment, see how he'd respond, "but she's been worried about the Freshman Junior thing," she bit the inside of her jaw and waited for his agreement or objection.

He leaned back in his chair, crossing his arms at his chest and feet at the ankles under the table and sighed, "It's not a big deal," he smiled.

Becca had the fight the urge to hug him. Just what she wanted to hear.

Mr. Dominick called the class to order just as she was about to ask him another question. Shockingly she found it easy to focus on class even with Jamie inches from her. She felt comfortable. Electric comfort. She would glance at him throughout class, sometimes catching his eye and exchanging smiles. By the end of third block Becca decided she had passed smitten and had moved onto something stronger.

"What do you have next?" Jamie asked in the final minute of class.

"Lunch," she smiled with sarcasm, "and then Biology. You?"

He returned her smile with a laugh, "Lunch and Physics. You and Emma sit with anyone at lunch?"

Becca swallowed her excitement and tried to keep her cool, "Not really. Most of the time we escape to the library for lunch. Less drama. Quieter," she shrugged, "you and Paul sit with the team?"

Jamie stood up when the bell rang and collected his books, "Most of the team have first lunch, so I just stick with Paul. But, uh," he flashed her a bright grin, "I had never thought of escaping. Mind if I tag along next time?"

She glanced at the door and saw Emma standing there watching them with an interesting grin on her face.

Becca turned her attention back to Jamie, "Of course you can. We don't go every day, but I'll find you next time."

"Great," he nodded and smiled shyly, "see you later," he gave a quick, nervous wave, and headed out the door, saying hello to Emma as he passed her.

Emma launched herself toward Becca, "What did he say?" she shrieked.

"He said he guessed he wouldn't have to wait to see me until tomorrow. He said that age doesn't matter. He has Physics next class. He's got our lunch and wants to go with us to the library next time. And," she took a deep breath, "he said that Paul likes you!" Becca could barely get the words out normally. She wanted to scream the news.

"No!" Emma gasped, clenching the straps of her book bag, "What? How did that come up?"

Becca laughed as they walked toward the cafeteria, "Jamie asked if he could sit next to me or if you were, I said no, you had Computer Tech and he said Paul did too, he'd be happy, he likes you," she finished quickly, dodging people.

"I just can't believe it. Paul actually likes me?!" she was beaming and staring at her feet, "maybe that's why he sat next to me in Comp. I was totally shocked," she put together, "but, anyway, it sounds like Jamie was being pretty obvious. I told you he liked you! He was happy to see you, he sat next to you, he wants to hang out with you at lunch. For sure signs he's into you," Emma concluded as they reached the cafeteria and she handed Becca a tray.

"I really hope so. He is a really nice guy," she chose a turkey sandwich and some fries, "He's genuine, you know? That sounds dumb," she added a water bottle to her tray and followed Emma to the check out.

"Have you really never noticed him before?" Emma asked as she paid for her pizza slice, apple and diet soda.

Becca shook her head and followed Emma to an empty table, "Never! We must have had classes on the opposite side of the school the first part of the year because I would have remembered that smile."

Sitting beside each other eating slowly while they replayed the happenings of the morning, Becca casually scanned the cafeteria. She found the table of basketball players about five tables away from theirs. Jamie was seated at the end of the long table, beside Paul, lazily leaning over his tray.

"So are you going to say anything to Paul?" Becca asked Emma without taking her eyes off of Jamie's back.

"No way," she laughed.

"You want me to tell him?" Becca asked, her gaze still on Jamie.

"That's what best friends are for," Emma laughed again, "are you going to make me say something to Jamie for you?"

Becca shook her head and finally looked at her friend, "Nope. I want him to say something to me if he's interested. I don't want to push."

"What if he doesn't say anything?" Emma asked quietly biting into her apple.

Becca shrugged and looked dissatisfied, "Then I guess it isn't meant to be."

They finished their lunch without any contact from Paul or Jamie. Nor did they see them in the science wing on their way to Biology, which Becca had been counting on since Jamie had Physics, two doors down.

Sitting next to Emma on the cold, metal stools in the Biology room, Becca pouted. Not long, though, she wasn't one for self-loathing. But not seeing Jamie when she had so been looking forward to was a harder let down than she could have imagined.

She decided on changing the subject back to Emma. Seeing her best friend sparkle with possibility was better than her own excitement.

"Hey, if you and Paul get together he could give you a ride home so you wouldn't have to ride that smelly bus," she leaned over and whispered to Emma as Mr. Potter was going over the Biology objectives.

Emma leaned low on the stool and tucked her chin, "I hate that bus," she smiled.

Becca tapped her pencil against her textbook, letting her thoughts distract her when she realized what if Jamie didn't like her at all. What if this was all over reactive perception? Because he was nice and smiled at her and sat next to her that meant he liked her? He could have just been a nice guy. She had no evidence that he was interested. Just speculation.

Deflated, Becca sunk into her desk and forced her attention on the pages in front of her. She was good at pushing things to the back of her head and into a box when she needed to. She didn't want to get her hopes up until she had some proof. She had learned through experience with her father that when It came to guys, one day would be sunshine and the next would be clouds.

When the last bell of the day rang, Becca shoved her books in her bag and begrudgingly slung it on her back, following Emma out the door.

"End of day one. How would you grade it?" Emma asked as they filtered into the crowded hall.

"A freaking plus," Becca laughed, elbowing her friend, "I mean, really. Classes are cake, Paul likes you. I met Jamie. Pretty great day."

"Agreed," Emma sighed, "I'll call you later," she said as they reached the front of the school. Emma had to race to her bus while Becca usually sat out front on the low concrete wall separating the building from the parking lot waiting for her mother.

She found an empty spot and hopped up, straightening her shirt and laying her book bag down beside her. Her mother wasn't in the growing line of parents who came to pick their kids up, so Becca pulled out the first novel they were to read in English, *A Wizard of Earth Sea*.

Becca was half way through chapter one when she looked up to scan the line of cars. Her mother still hadn't come, which was normal. Between leaving work, getting Ben settled and getting to the school, she was usually one of the last ones to arrive. Becca didn't mind.

Glancing around the parking lot and the courtyard in front of the school, she spotted Jamie speaking to two boys she didn't know. She hadn't realized how many people in school she really had zero contact with. As Jamie laughed at something that was said, he lifted his eyes and met Becca's stare. She lifted her hand and waved with a smile before dropping her eyes back to her book. She didn't want to see what, if any, reaction he'd have.

She had read three whole lines when she heard Jamie call to her.

"Hey!" he was jogging up to her seat on the wall, "What are you reading?" he asked when he reached her, tilting her book cover enough to see the title and nodded, "oh," he smiled, "neat book, test is a little tough though."

"I'll keep that in mind," she thanked him and peered out over the parking lot. She hoped her mother would be hours late.

"I didn't see you in the science hall," he commented, hopping up on the wall next to Becca.

She smirked. He was close, closer than he had been all day. It suddenly felt like the temperature had raised twenty degrees. "Were you looking for me?" she asked cautiously. Her outgoing nature sometimes would get her into trouble. She hoped this wasn't one of those times.

Jamie shrugged and hung his head, "Maybe," he toyed.

"I didn't see you either," she admitted, staring at him.

He blinked his blue eyes quickly and failed at trying to hide his ever present smile, "Were you looking for me?" he shot back.

She gritted her teeth and closed her book, "What does it mean if I were?" she asked through her clenched teeth. She felt nervous being so point blank.

Jamie's laughter boomed as he smiled again, his cheeks red, his eyes dancing, "I guess I could ask why you were looking for me."

"You could," she matched his smile.

He held her gaze for a moment and broke laughing, "Why were you looking for me?" his voice was filled with laughter.

From what Becca could sense, this was a going good. She scanned the parking lot again for her mother and silently vowed to never complaint about her mother being late again.

Clearing her throat Becca could feel herself blush as she looked at him, "I was looking for you because I wanted to see you," she said slowly, unable to peel her eyes away from him, "you're pretty to look at," she laughed.

He matched her laugh, his eyes squinting. He leaned into her, "I was looking for you because I wanted to see you. You're pretty to look at," he repeated her words with red in his cheeks.

Becca gaged her entire interaction with Jamie Enders in under thirty seconds to determine that he was genuine. He wasn't messing with her, he wasn't going to laugh at her for how she felt. She wasn't exactly sure how she was so confident in her feelings for and about Jamie, but she went with it.

Becca moaned when she heard the car horn in front of her and Jamie. Turning slowly, she seen her mother behind the wheel of their Buick, smiling and waving. Becca held up a finger to signal her mother she'd be there in a minute.

Jamie hopped off the wall and grabbed his bag, glancing back at the idling Buick he stepped into Becca, "May I have your number?" he held out a pen and the corner of his notebook, she jotted her number down quickly, "Want to go to the game together Friday night?" the blush had returned to his cheeks.

"Sounds great," she agreed, "See you tomorrow!" she nearly fell of the wall.

Jamie jogged off, turned and waved as he reached his car and looked embarrassed and then disappeared behind the wheel.

"You coming or spending the night?" Mrs. McKenon called out from the car.

Grabbing her book bag, Becca floated to the car, climbing into the passenger seat, "Hello, Mom," she said slamming the door and staring at the spot Jamie had been moments before.

"Hello, Mom," Lydia laughed, "who was that guy?"

In most ways Becca was like her mother. Outspoken, outgoing and down to earth. Life with Mr. McKenon was never easy but Lydia always made it smooth. Deep down Becca believed her mother may have been bothered by her father's constant absence and range of temperament, but you'd never see that. Lydia was even and happy all the time.

"Jamie Enders," Becca answered astutely, "he's in my French class and Accounting class. He's a Junior, he has blue eyes and a great smile. He asked if I'd go with him to the basketball game Friday night," she turned to tickle one of Ben's feet, but he was sound asleep in his car seat.

Lydia gleamed at her daughter surely, "Jamie, huh? Did you just meet him today?" she continued, eyeing Becca.

"Yeah, I've never seen him before in school, which is odd. I don't know how I could have missed him," she sighed happily.

"He asked you out after just meeting you? Does he know you're fifteen?" Lydia pressed.

Becca turned to her and tilted her head, "Really, Ma? Of course he knows how old I am. He still seems interested."

"Oh, girl!" Lydia laughed loudly, "it's written all over you,"

"What is?"

"You're in love!"

"Ma!" Becca screeched, "I'm not in love, that's ridiculous."

Lydia shook a pink polished nail at her daughter, "Trust me Girl. It's love, I can see these things," she winked.

Becca laughed, settled into her seat and stared out her window, smiling. As she watched Oakwood pass by, she let her imagination roam with thoughts of Jamie and how excited she had been to feel so happy.

CHAPTER 2

Becca jumped up off of the window seat, "Ma!" she called out, "he's here!" she stood in front of the mirror hanging by the front door and checked her appearance. She had braided parts of her blonde hair to look like a headband across the top of her head. She wore her favorite jeans and a loose fitting knit tunic over a blue tank top. She borrowed some books from Emma to complete her look.

"We're coming," Lydia answered as she entered the living room with Ben on her hip, "keep it down, you don't want to wake your father," she shushed her daughter then smiled.

Becca rolled her eyes, "He's got enough in him to be out for a while," she mouthed off and looked at her understanding mother, "he's here!" she squealed again, with her voice lowered.

Jamie had asked Becca to the game on Monday. By Wednesday he was insistent upon picking her up and dropping her off. On Thursday he referred to it as a "date". When Jamie waved goodbye to her Friday after school, after waiting with her for Lydia to show up, Becca was certifiably head over heels.

She launched toward the door when Jamie knocked.

"Hi," she said bubbly when she opened the door to face Jamie's smile beaming at her, "come in."

Jamie said hello to her quietly and stepped inside.

"Jamie, this is my mom and my brother Ben. Mom, this is Jamie," Becca introduced them.

"Mrs. McKenon, it's great to meet you. Thank you for letting Becca go with me to the game tonight," he said politely, with his best smile, shaking her hand.

"It's nice to meet you, Jamie. I've heard so much about you," Lydia grinned wide, "Becca doesn't stop talking about you."

Becca matched her mother's wide, inflicting, grin, "Mom tends to pry and exaggerate," she said acidly.

"If I am a topic of discussion, I hope it is all good," Jamie said reaching out to tousle Ben's hair.

Lydia laughed, "Oh, yes, Becca seems quite fond of you."

"Mom also doesn't know what discreet means," she whispered, "we should go."

Jamie chuckled and turned to follow Becca out the door, "it was nice to meet you, ma'am," he flipped and turned again, "I'm pretty fond of her too," Jamie nodded before breezing out the door and to his car.

"You'll have to excuse my mother, she doesn't always think before she speaks," Becca blushed as Jamie opened the car door for her.

She climbed in and watched him round the front of the car and slide behind the wheel, "My mother is the same way, but it's far worse. Your mom is nice, friendly. Mine can be plain mean," he looked forlorn as he pulled out of the driveway.

Becca and Jamie talked the entire way to the school, as they walked into the gymnasium and as they searched for Emma.

Spotting her three rows from the top of the bleachers, they sprinted up to sit with her. Paul had invited Emma to watch him play. She had been absolutely beaming since he had extended his invitation.

"Hey, guys," she greeted happily, scooting over to make room for them to sit down.

"You look nice, Em," Becca smiled, whisking her hand over Emma's hair that she had let fall straight down her back.

"Thanks," Emma hugged her best friend.

Becca sat down next to Emma, Jamie on her other side.

As the game began and Emma and Jamie became immersed in the action, Becca once again let her thoughts roam, thinking how she couldn't quite believe how comfortable she was with Jamie. Even that first afternoon, and now only five days later, there was something between them that was natural. Being with Jamie, talking to him, spending time with him, fit perfectly with Becca. She felt just as at ease with him as she did with Emma. Considering the amount of time Jamie had spent with her, she was beginning to think he felt the same way about her. He'd meet her in the morning when Lydia dropped her off, walked her to most of her classes, ate lunch with her and Emma and would wait with her until Lydia picked her up each afternoon. Things had changed for Becca in the last five days and she was excited.

"So, uh, what are you doing tomorrow night?" Jamie asked, raising his voice to where Becca could hear him. The crowd in the gym was cheering loudly for the home team.

Becca smiled to herself and leaned into his side, realizing this was the first physical contact they'd shared, "Going out with you, I think."

Jamie boomed with laughter and nodded before leaning into her as well. She felt what seemed like fire course through her body.

"Dinner and a movie?" He was watching the game but still leaning into her.

"Sounds great," she agreed.

He turned to her briefly, to exchange excited smiles and then returned his attention to the court. He stayed leaning against her side for the rest of the game.

CHAPTER 3

Staring at the night sky, watching the stars' twinkle and the dark clouds skate across the moon, Becca took a deep breath and exhaled slowly as she tucked her hands underneath her knees.

She was seated on a bench along the path in the neighborhood park. Jamie beside her. Earlier in the evening they had dinner at a small café in town and went to a movie, now they were concluding their night. In a small town like Oakwood with shops, eateries and the mall closed before your curfew, there wasn't a lot to do.

The park was only blocks from Becca's home and she knew it well. The night was warm and comfortable. Jamie had been quiet for a few minutes which let Becca sift through her thoughts.

Jamie was magnetic. She wanted to be around him all the time. To be near him, to listen to him. His presence was an energy that Becca enjoyed. They had known each other for only a week and a few people had already told them they acted as if they had been friends for years.

Friends. That's all they were, but Becca was wanting more. She had never had a boyfriend before, however something about Jamie was right to her. Jamie was flirtatious, polite and sweet. Most of the guys she encountered at school were not those things. Jamie was something different, something special.

"You're grinning. What are you thinking about?" Jamie interrupted with a small laugh.

Becca turned to look at him and smiled wider, "How great this has been," she nodded, "I've had fun," she adverted his eyes, which frightened her. She normally wasn't afraid or intimidated by looking anyone in the eye. Jamie was making her feel differently though.

"It has been fun," he agreed, looking at the sky.

Silence. Becca was normally uncomfortable in silence. It was one of the reasons she was so outgoing, to fill the silence. However, silence with Jamie felt like a warm blanket keeping her safe.

In the quiet, next to Jamie, staring at the endless sky, she sighed. Jamie matched her sigh and looked at her.

"Will you be my girlfriend?" he asked, then immediately shattered the quiet night with a laugh that seemed to roll, "that sounds so corny, but there is really no other way to say it, you know?" he was grinning and looking at her kindly.

She wanted to squeal, but held her excitement for a moment.

"The two years doesn't bother you?" she raised an eyebrow.

His forehead creased and he answered immediately, "Not at all. Does it bother you?"

"Not at all," she laughed.

"Good," he nodded, still looking at her, "so, is that a yes?"

She looked over his face, "Yes it's a yes."

Jamie sat up briskly, happiness spreading over him. He went to kiss her, but stopped short.

In a split second Becca decided he didn't get to be that close to her and not kiss her. She met his lips and kissed his smile easily. Like pieces of a puzzle, they fit just right.

Parting they shared a laugh again and laced their fingers together, sinking into each other's sides on the bench. They stayed just like that until it was close to curfew. They talked about school, families and their plans for the future. She told him things about her father that no one but Emma had known. He told her how unemotional his mother was.

Jamie drove her home and walked her to the door, kissing her again and saying goodnight. He promised to call her the next day. Becca waited outside until his car was completely out of sight before quietly entering the house. Her father's truck wasn't in the driveway so she assumed he was gone.

"Hey," Lydia greeted. She was sitting on the sofa in the darkened living room with the television on, the volume barely audible, "how did it go?" she asked enthusiastically, patting the couch for Becca to sit next to her.

"Were you waiting up for me?" Becca asked, plopping down next to her mother.

"Honestly, I wasn't. Ben gave me some trouble getting to sleep so I figured I'd just stay up a little longer, make sure he was good and out," she grinned, "so, how was it?"

Becca reviewed the entire date; the quiet dinner, the funny movie, the conversation in the park.

Lydia smiled and twisted a tendril of Becca's hair around her finger, "Don't worry about his mother. She'll love you."

They were silent for a moment. Becca closed her eyes and sighed, "How do you know when you're in love, Ma?"

Lydia stifled a laugh, "Girl, I think it's different for everyone. But I think it goes something like feeling you suddenly can't live without that person. They are all you'd ever need in life. They make you happy, they make you safe. They are your rock," she looked at her daughter, "you'll know with the whole of your heart when it hits you."

Becca processed what her mother said and looked up meekly, "I think I love him."

"Think?" she let the laughter ease out, "Oh, girl. I'm sure you do. I can see it, in both of you. Love is growing."

Becca reveled in her mother's words and then giggled, "Some people would say you're crazy, Ma."

"Call me crazy then," she sighed, "but I'm right."

Becca laughed again, smiling widely. She couldn't argue with her mother. As insane as it was, she wanted to believe every word. She had fallen for Jamie and she knew he was feeling the same.

Heading to her bedroom, Becca somehow felt confident and secure that Jamie Enders would forever change her life. And she loved that fact.

CHAPTER 4

"Emma!" Becca hissed as she whirled around. Emma had been mumbling objections to Becca's plan and she was becoming annoyed. Emma stopped in her tracks and took a step back. "It's an hour after curfew," Becca continued, "the house is dark. Dad is home and no one is awake. I'm not going in the front door to get caught, now come on," she grabbed Emma's reluctant hand and proceeded on the path around the back of the house.

The girls had been out on a date with Jamie and Paul and had lost track of time. Emma had permission to stay the night with Becca, but neither of them had permission to miss curfew. Mr. McKenon was uncharacteristically home and if he had been awakened, breaking curfew would be the least of their problems.

Becca reached her bedroom window and slowly eased it open. Quietly she leaned in and surveyed the room. Pitch black, door closed, and empty. The window was about mid-chest to Becca and she could easily hoist herself up onto the ledge and into the room. However, Emma was shaking from nerves and needed help.

"I'll give you a step," Becca said cupping her hand, "you'll ease right in."

Emma slapped her hand over her mouth to stifle a nervous laugh, "Are you serious?"

"It's this or walk home because I'm not waking my dad," Becca said firmly.

"Fine," Emma huffed. She tossed their purses into the room and stepped her right foot into Becca's cupped hands. She readied for the push, and Becca almost catapulted her onto the ledge, landing on the sill with a thud. She slid into the room easily, "hurry up!" she squeaked.

It took Becca two tries to lift herself onto the sill and into the room. She closed the window slowly and flicked on her bedside lamp, "Change fast, in case someone wakes up," she ordered, pulling the blinds down over the window.

Becca turned her back, peeled off her clothes and got into her pajamas in record time.

Sitting on the bed and brushing her hair, Emma asked, "Seems like you've done this before?"

Becca shrugged, "Twice. So far."

"You've been dating for a week!" Emma squealed quietly, "how come you're always late?"

Becca shrugged again, "I don't want to leave him. We get lost in conversation and before I know it, it's midnight. Now I just leave the window open enough for me to work it. I only really have to worry about it if Dad is home. Mom doesn't care too much, but he'll lose his mind."

Emma nodded in understanding and changed the subject, "Tonight was so amazing," she tossed her hair brush onto her overnight bag and clasped her hands together, "you and Jamie just fit. Paul is perfect," she fused.

"I agree," Becca smiled wide, "I feel like I've known Jamie forever. I love how Paul is so shy around you and protective," she laughed, "I hope it all stays like this."

"Me, too," Emma sighed, laying down on the bed and stretching, "We need some good in this life."

Becca had her obvious family issues, but Emma had a different set of circumstances. Her parents had moved to Paris two years ago to teach at a college there. They didn't want to uproot Emma from school or her life in Oakwood, so they decided to leave her here in the care of her grandmother. Emma missed her parents terribly, but got a long great with her grandmother. Emma's intentions were to graduate high school and move to Paris to attend college where her parents taught. The girls were sick about someday being separated, but knew that their lives would move along whichever course was meant for them.

Becca flinched into action when she heard footsteps in the house. Leaning behind her she flicked the bed side lamp off while Emma frantically scrambled underneath the covers. Becca slid in beside her and rolled her back to the door when it creaked open.

For added embellishment, Becca snored lightly and sighed, stretching under the covers and kicking Emma's shin. Whoever had opened the door quietly shut it and disappeared back down the hall.

Emma unleashed a laugh into Becca's back, "You had to snore? I was about to bust," she whispered.

Becca rolled onto her back and smiled, "Had to make it believable," she giggled, shrugging.

"Go to sleep," Emma laughed with one last giggle.

Becca laid awake wondering where her relationship with Jamie would lead, where it would end up taking her. She loved her mother and Ben, she even loved Emma, but at some point she wanted to be able to get away and be on her own. For the last few days she'd been praying Jamie would be there with her.

CHAPTER 5

Becca took another deep breath and glanced sideways at Jamie. He'd been uncommonly quiet for most of their date, leaving Becca to keep up the conversation. She had wondered what was keeping him quiet. They had yet to encounter a situation where they didn't immediately open up to each other about things that were bothering them.

Jamie hadn't acted different in any other way, besides the overwhelming quiet, so Becca decided whatever it was nagging at him would come out sooner or later.

As she drummed her fingertips on her knee she hoped it would be sooner. Silence was usually an enemy and silence from Jamie was beginning to make her nervous.

"Alright," her nervousness exploded, "what is it?" she clasped her hand together and turned slightly to face Jamie as he drove her home.

He abruptly looked at her, surprised by her sudden break of the silence air, "what are you talking about?" he questioned.

Becca laughed nervously, "You've been pretty quiet all night. Something on your mind? Maybe I could help? Or if something is up with me, you could tell me," she rambled a bit and took a breath as she focused on his changing smile.

"I'm sorry," he apologized, "there are just some things I've been thinking through, nothing to worry about," he smiled at her and placed a hand on her knee, "I should have said something sooner. I didn't mean to worry you."

Becca nodded, "It's alright," she smiled. If he didn't' want to divulge details of whatever he was working out, he didn't have to.

The rest of the ride home was silent. Becca cracked her knuckles and kept her hands busy. She hated silence.

Pulling up in front of Becca's house, she wanted to dart out of the car and into the house. She was upset with herself that she wanted away from Jamie, but him being so odd scared her. Even with his assurance.

Jamie escorted her out of the car and onto the front porch before her nervousness exploded again. Stopping on the steps, she pulled his arm, causing him to wheel around and face her as he stood two steps ahead of her, "What are you thinking through? You've got to tell me or I'm going to lose my mind."

Jamie grinned again, "You didn't do anything," he reiterated and gripped both of her hands, "look," she sighed and laughed, "I've been thinking a lot about you and me and what we're doing," he paused, letting her hands drop and wrapping her in a hug.

Becca felt better just being held by him, so she melted into his arms, resting her hand on his chest.

A moment passed, then two and Becca felt Jamie kiss the top of her head lightly and he rested his chin there.

"I love you, Becca," his voice was uneven as he skated across the words.

Becca felt herself stiffen and her brain shot into overdrive.

HE LOVED HER?!

"I know it hasn't been that long, but I also know what I feel. When I am with you, nothing else matters, it's just you. I've been trying to think of the perfect way to tell you."

Becca nodded and reached up to kiss him. But she didn't say anything. And she didn't know why. Everything inside her screamed that she loved him, too. She wanted to tell him so badly, but something held her mouth closed.

He hugged her tightly and somehow she knew there was no pressure to say anything in return.

She felt blissful. Jamie loved her. This is what true love felt like, looked like. She knew she loved him. She also knew that life could change at any given second for the good or the bad, so cherishing moments that meant the most were pertinent.

CHAPTER 6

Becca paced back and forth in front of the school. Classmates were being dropped off and filtering in from the student parking lot. She was watching attentively, waiting for Jamie to pull into the lot. She been there for fifteen minutes, eyeing the entire lot.

She had decided that morning that today was The Day. She and Jamie had been together three weeks now. Thirteen days ago he had told her he loved her. And since, she had wrestled with how and when to tell him she felt the same way.

At breakfast she had confided in her mother her feelings. Her mother told her to follow her heart, but to let him know either way. He was probably waiting. She may have been only fifteen years old, but she was certain this, Jamie, was what the rest of her life would hold.

Becca snapped back to the present from her recollection of that morning's conversation when Jamie pulled into the lot.

She hesitated for a split second and then sprinted through the lot, weaving between groups of students and cars pulling in and parking. She glided around the back of Jamie's car as he climbed out, slinging his book bag on his shoulders.

"Jamie," she greeted him, her voice higher, louder than she had intended.

He jumped from surprise, then laughed, "you scared me!"

"Sorry," she heaved, trying to catch her breath.

"You ran out here?" he looked her over, "everything okay?"

She nodded, sucking in air, "I ah, just," she stopped and held a finger up, signaling him to give her a minute.

Closing her eyes, she took deep breaths until she was breathing normally. Opening her eyes, Jamie was staring at her with an interesting smile across his face.

"What?" his forehead creased as he locked his car.

Becca reached up and cupped his face with both her hands, "I love you Jamie. I mean it. I don't know why I waited so long to say it. I love you. Always."

She watched his eyes dance as she spoke, their corners reached upward as his smile widened.

He gripped her quickly and tightly and kissed her deeply. Not like he had in front of anyone before. Neither of them seemed to care who could be watching, judging. In that moment, they were engulfed in love, in each other.

"I love you always, huh?" he repeated back to her.

She dropped her hands and wrapped her arms around his waist, "I love you always. Forever."

Jamie nodded with a wide smile, "I love you always then," he laughed and kissed her again, just as deeply, just as sweet.

"You had me worried," he admitted when they parted.

"I'm sorry. I don't know why I didn't scream it back at you immediately," she laughed.

Jamie slipped an arm around her shoulders and led her toward the building, "I'm happy now," he kissed her temple.

Becca snaked her arms around his waist as they walked, "Always," she whispered as the crossed the entrance of the school and met up with Paul and Emma.

She couldn't explain why or how, but she felt completely certain that Jamie would be a part of her life forever. Like they said, it was for Always.

CHAPTER 7

Becca's head was swirling and she felt as if she had just been annihilated.

"Mother, really," Jamie huffed, crossing in front of Becca who was seated on the couch. He stood slightly in front of her, "you're not going to change my mind," he paused, "neither of you are going to change my mind," he laughed, "if it isn't something we can work through, I'll move out," he said pointedly as he finished and sat down beside Becca, placing an arm around her shoulders gently.

Becca had attempted to tune out most of the conversation especially since it had begun to go south. Jamie had just told his parents his plans for the future. He had graduated two weeks prior and they had been pushing him to choose and apply to a college. He had decided long before graduation that he would wait for Becca to finish high school and they'd attend college together. Being ahead of her by two years hadn't created many obstacles, until now.

His parents were not very understanding. Mr. Enders had always been sensitive to Becca and Jamie's relationship. Probably because Mrs. Enders was the complete opposite. She had never approved of Becca, never accepted her. She barely tolerated her. And now, her only child, withholding his life to wait for her? Mrs. Enders had made it noticeably clear that she was not happy, that it was Becca's fault and that Jamie was making mistake after mistake.

Mr. Enders cleared his throat, "Have you thought this through son?"

"Of course I have," Jaime responded immediately.

"If you are set on waiting, I'll have to insist on some standards."

He stopped speaking when Mrs. Enders gasped so loudly it startled him.

"Michael!" she hissed, "you're just going to accept this?"

All eyes were on Mr. Enders.

He shrugged, "Carol, Jamie is an adult, he can make his own decisions. If this is what he wants, fine. All decisions have consequences and breed experience," he was looking at Jamie and spoke sternly, "you wait for College, fine. You will work in the meantime. You can stay here also. I probably can find you something at the firm. You'll save portions of your pay to go toward school. You'll still have your curfew and house rules. And if for any reason this goes south," he pointed a finger between Jamie and Becca, "you apply to schools immediately."

Becca didn't think his suggestions were all that terrible. She had tried talking Jamie out of waiting herself, but there was no use. It was him and her together or not at all.

She looked up at Jamie who smiled warmly at her. She nodded at him and clenched his hands.

"Deal," he agreed, smiling at his father, "two years of work experience will be great," Jamie nodded.

Carol huffed once more and stormed out of the room.

It was no secret, from the very beginning, over a year ago, that Carol Enders had an utter distaste for Becca and she didn't bother to hide it or downplay it. It was well known to everyone involved that Carol thought Becca wasn't good enough for Jamie.

It bothered Lydia more than it bothered Becca, the loathing. Becca had let it get to her as little as possible. She couldn't do anything about it, she couldn't change her mind. Short of walking away from Jamie nothing Becca did would make Mrs. Enders happy. She accepted that and moved with it. She cared about Jamie and that was her only concern. Jamie loved her no matter what either of his parents said and nothing was going to change that.

"I apologize, Becca, for Carol's behavior. She's always been protective of Jamie and held high expectations for him," Michael explained, like he had to do many times before. He slapped a hand down on Jamie's shoulder, "I'm proud of you, son, for following your own path and standing your ground," he said with a hushed whisper, "don't mind your mother," he patted Jamie's shoulder and hurried toward the back of the house, no doubt in an attempt to find and calm down Carol.

"She's absolutely despises me!" Becca sighed, shaking her head.

Jamie smacked his lips together, "She despises everyone," he nudged her, "if she didn't give birth to me, she'd probably despise me too," he rolled his eyes and smiled, "I'm such a disappointment."

Becca looked his face over, "Are you really sure about this? I'm causing all kinds of problems."

"Certainly," he didn't hesitate, "like Dad said, don't mind her. She'll live. Listen, I'm not leaving you. I want to start that chapter with you, on the same level. Two years is nothing," he paused to kiss her, "however, I do have to make a request. Can we please move the hell away from here for college? I need a break."

Laughing Becca agreed, "Mom practically ordered me to go to school out of state. Told me I needed to see the world, build experience, and then if I wanted, come back home,"

"See, this is why I love your mother. She gets it. Mom is only concerned with how it'll look. Her son, wasting away his life with his under aged girlfriend, waiting around for her. She's such a horrible influence!" he laughed.

"I do manage to talk you into things you probably wouldn't otherwise agree to," she kissed him now, coyly.

Jamie laughed and blushed, "Just that one thing. And you didn't really have to talk me into doing that. I kind of was already on board."

"I just pushed you over," she whispered, "what if your mother knew that?"

"Pretty sure it would kill her, so let's just keep it to ourselves," his hands were intertwined with hers. He was smiling widely at her.

Becca laughed, "Ourselves, Emma and my mother."

He gasped, startled, "You told your mother?"

"She can read me like a book! The second I walked in the door that night she called me out. I'm serious, I didn't even say 'hey mom' and she was like 'oh, I know what you did'. It was terrifying," Becca tried hard not to laugh at Jamie's stricken expression.

"I can imagine," he sighed, pulling her toward him and wrapping her in his arms, "I love you always."

"Always," Becca nodded. In his arms she felt the most comfortable, the safest.

CHAPTER 8

"Emma, do you have the glue stick?" Becca lifted and shuffled pieces of paper, pictures and the book balancing in her lap.

"Here," she answered from her seat at Becca's desk. She tossed the glue stick to her best friend with a smile, "we should have grabbed two of those."

Becca shrugged and slathered some glue on the back of a picture before slapping it on the open page of the scrapbook she was working on, "oh well," she quipped, capping the glue and dropping it next to her scissors.

The girls had decided to make scrapbook recollecting their high school years and would trade them with each other after graduation. It was only a week away and it was becoming painfully clear life was about to change.

Emma was leaving for Paris two day after graduation. Becca had no idea when, or if ever, she'd see her best friend again. She was sad she wouldn't be attending college with Emma, but she was overjoyed with her own plans. She'd studied hard, achieved a high enough grade point average to receive a full scholarship; the only conceivable way she would be able to attend college.

She and Jamie had applied to several schools, but were both accepted to Colorado State University. Across the country. Just what Jamie and her mother had hoped for. Jamie had saved quite a bid from his job over the last two years to secure a private dorm room in one of the newer additions to the campus. Becca had been assigned to a suite room in a different dorm, sharing with one other girl. Becca had plans to inform her roommate that she wouldn't be there too often, if at all. Jamie's dorm had no restrictions on guests they had decided they wanted to try living together. The parents didn't know that detail, and right now, didn't need to.

"Hey, look at this one?" Emma held up a photo of Becca and Jamie then flashed it back to herself, "remember, that was you're first 'date'?" Emma laughed, "Ug, Paul is in the background," she huffed rolling her eyes.

Becca laughed, glaring at her friend through her eyelashes, "Still hanging on to that?" she asked.

Emma sailed the photo across the room to Becca, "I just don't know how I could have been so wrong, you know?"

When Jamie and Becca had gotten together, so had Emma and Paul, sort of. They were much less serious. When the boys graduated, Paul went off to college in Arizona and soon stopped all contact with Emma, and even Jamie. Doing some digging, Jamie found out he'd begun dating someone he'd met at school and decided to avoid letting anyone know. Including Emma.

She was heartbroken, but moved on pretty quickly. She dated a few other classmates in the last two years, but nothing serious. She focused on school and was counting down to starting over in Paris.

"He got us all really," Becca said, pasting the picture into her book and placing a sticker over Paul's body.

Emma nodded her head, "That was a long time ago," she murmured.

Nearly three years had gone by since Jamie and Becca had met. They had grown very close in that time, their relationship was strong, concrete. Becca had no doubts, from the very beginning, the validity of Jamie's feelings for her. From day one, they had been inseparable.

After Jamie graduated he began to pick up and take Becca to school each morning on his way to work and pick her up every afternoon. He'd spend most evenings with Becca. They hardly ever fought and complimented each other well. Jamie had even attended Becca's Junior and Senior Proms.

She was excited about their future; college, living together, living away from home, starting a career and life goals. Her life prior to Jamie was a distant memory and stayed planted in a far corner of her mind.

"Oh," Emma jumped slightly in her seat and jerked toward Becca, "remember this?" she asked flicking a piece of paper folded into an arrow between her thumb and forefinger.

Becca cocked her head to the side and narrowed her eyes, "Didn't we fold notes like that Freshman year?" she recounted.

Emma nodded, "Right, but this note is one you wrote to me the night of your first date," her expression was joyful, "remember you got home late and couldn't call me so you wrote everything down and then brought it to me the next day?" she carefully unfolded the note, "I read this a million times," she glanced over the page and then taped it into the book she was working on.

Sighing loudly, Becca tried to push Emma's departure out of her mind. Her stomach had been in knots while they were working on the scrapbooks, remembering all their good times. Knowing there wouldn't be many more.

"I honestly hate that you're leaving," Becca announced, not looking at her friend.

Emma was quiet for a moment and then sighed herself, "If it's any consolation it was a very hard decision, besides," she paused, "with me gone you'll be able to spend every waking second with Jamie," she balled up a piece of paper and threw it at Becca, "we'll make it," she assured.

Becca had hoped their friendship would survive a continent change and an ocean apart. Somewhere deep inside her heart she knew it would never be the same. She had mindlessly decided that Jamie would now not only be her love, but her best friend, her happiness and her entire life.

Lydia had informed her of the implications of placing all you have in one person, but quickly realized Becca's mind, and heart, had been made up.

The unexpected barging in of Ben was enough for the girls to take a break from their project. Ben had become meticulous at opening doors now and was all the happier to see what everyone was doing.

"Sissy!" he screeched and clumsily climbed atop Becca's bed and into her now empty lap, "Momma says Jams here!" he held his hand up.

Emma laughed at him and closed her book.

"OK, Ben, tell him he come in," Becca kissed the top of his head and he just as clumsily climbed off the bed. His little voice boomed through the house as he let Jamie and probably the neighbors, know that Jamie could "come on back".

Becca slid the remaining papers and pictures into the front of the scrapbook and laid it on her night stand.

"Hello," she heard Jamie say as he tapped on the door, "Ladies," he greeted, smiling at Emma and dutifully sitting beside Becca on the bed. He leaned in for a kiss as soon as he was seated.

"Hi," he whispered to Becca, casually rubbing her back.

When Jamie was in the room, life became exponentially better.

"So what have you been up to today?" Becca asked, leaning back into his hand.

Jamie sighed, "Ran copies for Dad most of the morning, he has a trial starting Monday. Then mom tried to con me into moving around furniture when I got home," he rolled his eyes, "I'm truly amazed at the mindless things she comes up with to try and get me to stay home," he shook his head and looked to Emma, "she guilt tripped both me and Dad into cleaning the garage tomorrow," he sighed.

"Maybe I'll stop by," Becca shrugged, laughing with Emma.

"Please do," he laughed, "not only to see you, but to see her expression. Here she thinks she's got a surefire way to hole me up all day," he sighed and paused, "August can't get here quick enough."

Jamie and Becca were slated to move to Colorado the second week in August to get ready to start school at the beginning of September. Most of Becca's room had been packed and boxes lined her walls. They sat and talked most of the afternoon, reminiscing as Becca and Emma continued working on their scrapbooks. Emma educated them on Paris, Jamie likewise about Colorado. Becca kept quiet and observed mostly. Days like these were numbered and she wanted to enjoy them as much as possible.

CHAPTER 9

Becca groaned and then laughed as Jamie shook her foot from the end of the bed, "No," she moaned in response, "I just want to lay here for the rest of my life," she whined, rolling over onto her stomach.

Jamie continuously rapped on the sole of her tennis show, "If we unload the car now we'll have all weekend to lay around," he said, his voice amused by her childlike actions.

Shaking her head into the pillow, she laughed harder, "How are you not exhausted? I'm absolutely beat," she rolled back over, "nearly thirty hours in that car! Seventeen hundred sum-odd miles," she sighed, "and two flights of stairs into this place!" she waved her hand about the small room, "and you're still raring to go."

Jamie looked around the room with a smile on his face, "I'm excited. Granted I'll probably pass out later, but for right now," he stood beside Becca and nudged her until she shifted to give him enough room to sit down, "I just want to get it all done and have the rest of the time to enjoy it."

Becca whined for a few more minutes before Jamie got up and pulled her to her feet.

"I hate your car, by the way," she mumbled, following him out of the apartment and back down the two flights of stairs and into the parking lot.

They had driven across county to CSU in Fort Collins, Colorado to start their college experience, over the last day and a half, stopping only for food and restroom breaks, taking turns driving so the other could sleep.

Once on campus they easily found Jamie's apartment building, part of the International on campus apartments. Jamie had originally, once he and Becca had been accepted, prepaid for a private dorm room in which he'd share with Becca under a guest pass. However, after orientation he had decided that the on campus apartments would work out better. The rules were more flexible, the apartments were more spacious and closer to campus.

In May, Becca had been assigned to a separate dorm but after confiding in her mother she and Jamie's plans to live together, she withdrew her dorm request, telling Housing that she'd be living in the campus apartments. Jamie had transferred his prepaid dorm account to the prepaid apartment and was paid through Sophomore year.

They had brought little with them for the college inception. The apartment was relatively small, but came furnished. Becca and Jamie brought their most precious possessions, packed his Ford Focus and headed off to start their lives together.

After seven trips from the apartment to the car, there were boxes and bags scattered all over the one-bedroom apartment.

"See," Jamie sighed, rolling up his sweater sleeves to his elbows, and plopping down on the couch, "all done."

Becca stood with her hands on her hips by the front door, "Yeah, right. You know me better than that. You know I can't just leave all this stuff hanging around. I'll have them unpacked tonight."

Jamie grinned wickedly and nodded, "My evil plan worked," he said dramatically, kicking his heels up on the little coffee table.

"You have ten minute to catch your breath and then you start helping" Becca called out, disappearing into the adjacent bedroom.

"I'll start with the coffee maker," he yelled back to her with a laugh.

Giggling to herself, she began unpacking as much as she could. The bedroom was furnished with a Queen sized bed and two nightstands. The closet was smaller than the one she had at home. Surveying the empty spaces in the bedroom Becca decided they needed a dresser and bookshelf at least. As she filled half of the restricted closet with her clothes, half with Jamie's she could hear him unpacking in the kitchen and could smell coffee brewing.

"We need to go shopping," Becca called out as she quickly made the bed.

"You're not kidding," Jamie answered as he clanged cabinets shut, "We don't have a toaster. We need a toaster."

Becca nodded and made a quick list in her head as she lined the remaining bags against the wall. She had no more room for the remaining clothes, the books and other smaller items they had brought.

"We'd need food to use a toaster," she sighed returning to the kitchen that openly joined the living area.

"Exactly," Jamie nodded, pointing a stack of plates he was holding at her before sliding them onto a shelf.

"And a dresser, bookshelf and something for that balcony," she pointed over her shoulder, "it's a decent size and nice."

Jamie smiled at her sweetly, "Patio set, check. I'll get the TV hooked up if you want to do the bathroom?" he stood in the center of the kitchen, his hands on his hips.

"Sounds good," she located the boxes of toiletries and began arranging the tiny bathroom while Jamie assembled the modest entertainment center and placed the TV appropriately.

It didn't take them long to get the apartment to their liking and make a list of what they needed.

"How will this all fit in your car?" Becca asked. She leaned against the bar where Jamie was seated on a stool.

"May have to make trips or find someplace that delivers. We can get boxed stuff, put it together ourselves."

Letting her laugh flow Becca raised an eyebrow, "Do you have tools for that?"

Jamie looked at her strangely, "Of course not," he roared with laughter, "add it to the list."

"Alright," she pulled on his hand, "let's go, I'm getting hungry."

The campus was a sprawling mass in the foothills below a wall of mountains far on the horizon. It was at least five miles from the school to the nearest bustling of stores, offices, banks and restaurants. From their balcony they could see out over the plains of the campus and to the lights of Fort Collins. It was overwhelmingly quiet.

Finding a small deli across the street from a Wal-Mart, they ate a quick dinner and crossed the street to start checking items off their list. With everything but the patio set purchased they were satisfied and headed back. Jamie's car had been packed to its utmost limit, the trunk having to stay open with the boxed dresser and book shelf sticking out of it.

"I'm glad we don't have to go far or fast," he whistled as he tied down the boxes, "poor car."

Back at the apartment, hilarity ensued as Jamie became acquainted with the new power tools and how to piece together the new, faux wood furniture. It was well into the early morning hours when all they had purchased was put together and the last box been unpacked.

Jamie had showered and changed into a pair of lounge pants and a shirt while Becca finishing folding and placing the remaining clothes in the dresser.

"I'm not entirely sure that thing will hold up," Jamie warned rubbing a towel over his damp hair, as Becca placed items on the dresser top.

Laughing, she gathered up her pajamas, "I think it will, you did good," she assured him before disappearing into the bathroom herself.

After her shower, Becca climbed into their bed, next to Jamie. He'd already huddled underneath the covers and was leaning against the headboard, looking through the course description magazine.

"I think it finally hit me," she said, laying down to lean on his chest.

Jamie tossed the magazine onto the night stand and wrapped his arms around her, "What did?"

"This. Being away from home. Being on our own," she paused, "I'm scared."

Finally, being alone for more than five minutes since they left Oakwood, Becca had started to feel anxious in the shower. Fear set in quickly as she began to question if they were ready, if she were ready, for what was about to begin.

Jamie rubbed his hands along her arms and kissed the top of her head, "I'm scared, too, but I'm also excited. We're going to be fine, everything will go great. I miss home, too, but this is what we wanted," he paused then and cleared his throat, "this is what you wanted right?"

"Of course," Becca assured him, nodding against his chest, "it's just so different. So fast. It's real."

She knew exactly what was bothering her, as did Jamie. She missed her mom and Ben. Her free spirit had agreed with her mother that she attend college out of state, to live a different life, to have experiences she wouldn't otherwise have. At the time she hadn't really thought about what it would feel like when it started. How much she missed her family was surprising.

"I know Becca, but it'll be alright. I'm sure your mom misses you too, but she's really happy about this, you know? You getting to do something she never could. She's proud of you."

Becca nodded again and unwillingly let the tears fall.

"We can go back at any moment you want," Jamie added, "I'm serious. We're not doing this if it makes you miserable. I won't let you be unhappy."

"I am happy," Becca interjected, "I'll be okay in a few days," she promised.

They were quiet for a while. Becca's life long fight against silence had ended over the summer. Silence with Jamie felt like every other minute, it no longer scared her or made her uncomfortable.

"We're doing this together. I'm here for you," Jamie said softly after a few minutes.

Becca squeezed him tight, "I know. You are what is making this worthwhile," she said kissing his chest, "I love you."

"Always," he said leaning his chin on the top of her head as he continued to hold her tightly.

CHAPTER 10

Becca smirked loudly in the empty stairwell. The sound of her laughter echoed against the bright yellow concrete walls.

"You're serious, Emma? His name is Remi? R-E-M-Y?" she paused, balancing her bag on her left shoulder, the cell phone on her right, "oh, I'm, sorry, Remi. So, what's he like? I have to remember there probably aren't that many Mark's or Jason's in Paris."

"He's gorgeous Becca! He's a little taller than me, green eyes, and dirty blond hair that's kind of long. Enough where he can put it behind his ears or pony it. He's slim, he's in the drama club and his accent is to die for!"

Becca laughed again to herself as she continued to climb the second flight of stairs to her apartment, "And he's in your Biology class?"

"Yeah," Emma squeaked, "he's really nice Becca. He's been coming by every other night to help me with homework,"

Scoffing Becca leaned against the door that opened to her floor, holding it open for a group of students making their way downstairs, "You were an ace in Bio, you need help?"

"Hell, no, but he offered and I accepted. My parents really like him too," she said with fact.

"So is he on his way over now?" Becca asked gliding down the hallway.

"Should be here any minute, it's nearly seven now," she replied with excitement.

"Oh, well, I'll let you go then. Enjoy your evening and call me later on, let me know how it's going," Becca fumbled in her bag for her keys.

"I will. Tell Jamie I said hello and happy anniversary," Emma shrilled.

"Thank you, I will. Love you!" she sighed, fishing the keys out of the bottom of her overloaded bag.

"Jet'aime," Emma said before hanging up.

Becca slide her new cell phone closed and readjusted her bag before unlocking the front door.

"Jamie, I'm home," her voice caught in her throat when she looking into the apartment, "oh my God," she whistled with a smile. She habitually opened the front door, placed her bag and shoes on the floor, closed it and placed her phone and keys on the kitchen counter.

"Where are you?" she called out.

There were at least twenty candles lining the kitchen, along the coffee table and entertainment center. The room smelt of floral, cinnamon and chocolate. Two place settings were on the bar where they usually ate.

She and Jamie both got out of classes at twelve fifteen on Wednesday's and were both normally home by now.

Taking a few steps into the kitchen she could see Jamie on the balcony, his back to her.

"Hey," she said louder. This time he whirled around quickly, a look of shock on his face.

"I thought I'd be able to hear you come in," he said sliding the balcony door closed behind him.

"I called for you," she smiled at him, "what is all this?" she blushed.

When he reached her, Jamie gripped her hands and smiled his perfect smile, "Happy four-year anniversary," he said softly.

"You remembered," Becca laughed, melting into him for a hug.

"You've only been reminding me for the entire week," he chuckled, "of course I remembered, how could I forget?"

"This is romantic," Becca appreciated, "it's nice."

"Thank you," he sighed, kissing her, "it's only a piece of what I have planned."

Becca looked at him suspiciously, "what else have you got planned?"

Jamie's smiled widened across his face, causing his eyes to squint together, "a candle lit desert celebration," he waved a hand at the place setting at the bar, "a cozy afternoon spent in bed," his face reddened, "a romantic dinner out and this," he pulled a black velvet box from his back pocket.

"Jamie," Becca said, stunned, "I didn't get you anything," she bit her bottom lip, "does that make me a bad girlfriend?"

Jamie smirked, "The worst," he joked, "but I'm sure you'll figure something out. Go on, open it."

Embraced in Jamie's arms, Becca lifted the box top to reveal a white gold cable chain necklace with a white gold charm on it that had a small diamond in it, "Jamie, it's gorgeous!"

"Here," he took the necklace out of the box and slipped it around her neck, clasping it and straightening the charm over her collarbone, "now it's gorgeous."

"Thank you," Becca said hugging him tightly, "I love it. When do you have time to do all this?"

"I skipped Communications this morning and went out," he confessed.

"You skipped class for me?" she squeaked, "don't let your mother find out."

"She was right all along, you're such a terrible influence," he smirked.

Laughing, they parted and Becca sat at the bar while Jamie opened and sliced up two pieces of chocolate cake.

Sitting next to him as the ate, Becca thought about the past four years and all they had been through. Being with Jamie changed Becca. She wasn't as hard, as guarded, as she had been in the days before they had met. He steadied her, he loved her unconditionally and without judgment or expectation.

Enjoying every morsel of her anniversary cake, Becca looked forward to many more anniversaries with Jamie.

CHAPTER 11

The loud applause coming from their table could be heard through half of the restaurant. Becca lowered her head in embarrassment and scanned nearby tables. There were a few onlookers, but most were too immersed in their own conversations to even realize that seven members of the restaurants wait staff had just unwillingly sang Happy Birthday to a twenty-year-old.

"Do you feel twenty" Emma asked, leaning into Becca's side with a thud.

Becca thought for a moment, "Not really, I guess," she shrugged, "it sounds crazier than it feels."

"How do you like your birthday present?" Jamie asked, putting an arm around her shoulders and grinning wildly.

"You're fishing for compliments," Cassie pointed her cake covered fork at him from across the table.

"It was a great gift!" he said with laughter.

Secretly, Jamie had pulled together Becca's friends from school, Cassie and Vivian, and had Emma fly in from Paris to celebrate. When Emma arrived at the apartment shortly before dinner it was a complete shock. Perfect gift.

"You going to eat that?" Cassie asked Vivian, pointing the fork at Vivian's half eaten piece of cake.

Vivian slid the plate and leaned back in the booth, "Take it. I can't eat another bite."

Becca spent most of the dinner listening to her friend's conversations. Cassie and Vivian were impressed with Emma's foreign lifestyle and wanted to hear all about Paris. Emma was like wise interested in Colorado life and how Becca and Jamie had changed.

Jamie sat quietly, methodically rubbing Becca's shoulder. They never seemed to be disconnected from each other. They had changed, grown up, in the almost two years they been away at school.

Surviving on their own had made them stronger and rightly dependent on each other. They knew each other's every move, every quirk and every mood. They were inseparable if not for different class scheduled, but continued to grow together.

Becca was grateful to spend her birthday with her best friends, but she was more gracious for her relationship with Jamie. Jamie filled in every hole that was left. She was happy, content, with her life and her studies and hoped that the wonderful life she had now would never change.

"What are you thinking about?" Jamie whispered into her ear, startling her.

She smiled up at him and rolled her eyes, "How amazing you are and how I hope it's this perfect forever."

Jamie kissed her quickly and tightened his grip on her, "It will be. You deserve nothing less than a perfect life."

CHAPTER 12

Slowly, and with the help of Jamie, Becca heaved the gigantic turkey out of the oven, sliding it quickly onto the stove top.

"That's enough turkey to feed an army," Jamie muttered, his eyes wide, as he tossed the pot holders onto the counter.

"Mom has the tendency to go overboard," Becca explained, closing the oven and sighing, "we'll have leftovers all weekend."

"And then some," he nodded surveying the steaming bird.

"Ever carve one before?" Becca asked him with a smile.

Jamie looked perplexed for a moment and shrugged, turning his gaze to her, "Can't be that hard right?" he laughed.

"How did you guys do?" Lydia asked, coming into the small kitchen, "oh wonderful," she sighed happily when she seen the highlight of their Thanksgiving dinner.

"Need help with anything else?" Jamie asked moving around the kitchen effortlessly. The look on his face was of intense joy. He placed an arm around Becca as she came to stand beside him.

"If you want to start placing everything on the table, I'll get the gravy going and we should be set," Lydia answered.

Ben had made placemats at school with turkeys on them and they were neatly lined up on the dining room table.

Before long the small table was covered with the greatest smelling food that had graced Becca since being home over the summer.

Almost four months ago, she and Jamie had begun their Junior year of college. Classes were going extremely well and Jamie was able to re-up his agreement on the apartment through Graduation.

Over the summer they had flown home to visit their families.

Becca had spent most of her summer helping her mother clean out the house. Specifically removing the items her father has left behind when he finally left the family for good in April. It was no big surprise to Becca or her mother. It had been years in the making. He just didn't bother returning after one of his trips. A week later, divorce papers arrived in the mail. It was over in a matter of three months.

It was hardest on Ben, he was still young and still had hope Dad would actually be a Dad. For six years old he understood quite well what had happened, even promising to take care of his sister and mother when he grew up.

Their Thanksgiving dinner was small; Lydia, Becca, Jamie and Ben. Becca had no other family and Jamie's parents had regrettably declined Lydia's invitation to dinner. Jamie had spent the morning with them, but was soon back where he felt most comfortable; with Becca.

"You going to carve that bird for us Jamie?" Lydia asked, lurching the bird into the center of the table. She sighed when she sat down and smiled at him genuinely.

"Yes, ma'am, I'm going to try," he smiled graciously back, slightly embarrassed, "pretty sure our last few birds came in a box," he laughed.

Jamie's sheltered upbringing caused a lack of some common knowledge. Growing up there was always someone to do the harder things for him. Putting together an entertainment center in the apartment was a crowning achievement. Carving a holiday bird would be another. Just last month he managed to finally figure out how to change the oil in his car. He enjoyed learning these things that most men his age already knew. He was a self-proclaimed, accepted, late bloomer.

"Can I do it next year?" Ben asked, sitting straight up in his chair.

"You'll probably have to, buddy," Jamie laughed as he made his first incision.

Jamie laughed at himself with each cut, knowing his audience was readily observing every move. When a sufficient amount of meat was stacked neatly, he laid down the carving knife and took a bow.

"You're welcome," he said with a proud smile.

"Perfect," Becca said to him when he took his seat beside her. She leaned over and kissed his cheek gently.

Blushing and grinning wide, Jamie rolled his eyes at her and squeezed her knee under the table.

After a quiet dinner and team effort of cleaning everything up, Lydia joined Becca on the front porch to watch Jamie and Ben run around the front yard, kicking a soccer ball back and forth.

She handed Becca a cup of hot tea and sat down on the step beside her and laughed, "I think Ben was just as excited to see Jamie as he was to see you," she said, sipping her tea.

Becca nodded, not taking her eyes off of Jamie, "How is he doing?"

"Alright, I guess. He's stopped asking questions about him. He tries to help me with everything," she paused, "he's only six, he shouldn't be thinking like that," she sighed.

"He's perceptive," Becca nodded, finally turning toward her mother, "he's smart. He's seen how people should and shouldn't be treated. It's a lot for a child, but if he's adjusting well enough it should be okay," she shrugged, "we just really have to let him be a kid and to know we appreciate his protectiveness, but it's not his responsibility."

There was silence for a moment before Lydia spoke again, changing the subject, "How are things at school? With Emma? With Jamie?"

Becca laughed, "I can't believe we're Juniors already. It seems like we were just packing up and driving away," she smiled sweetly at her mother, "Emma is having a great time in Paris. She absolutely loves it. She and Remi are still together. I've never heard her so happy," she shook her head, "and Jamie and I are fine as always."

"Fine as always?" Lydia repeated, "that's all I get?"

Becca's laughter caused the boys to look up from their game to peer at her.

"What do you want?" she asked, smirking.

"Details, girl!" Lydia howled, "future plans, discuss anything about life after college?"

"We'll probably move back home," Becca shrugged.

"Back to Oakwood?" Lydia stopped, "that's all you've got? You'll graduate and move back to Oakwood."

"Oh," Becca whistled. She suddenly knew what her mother had been asking. Future plans meaning, marriage and children. "Aren't we a little young to get married?"

"You've been married since you were fifteen, when will you make it official?" Lydia pressed on through her laughter.

Becca shook her head, embarrassed.

It wasn't that the thought of marrying Jamie hadn't crossed her mind, it had. It had even been discussed once, but hearing someone else bring it up made it more real.

"Maybe you should ask Jamie. Isn't the guy supposed to pop the question?" Becca bit down on her bottom lip.

"Oh, these days it doesn't matter," Lydia waved, eyeing Jamie in the yard, "Seriously, though, has it been discussed?"

Becca sighed slowly and lowered her voice, "Once, but to no great extent. Trust me, Mom, when things start looking that way, you'll be the first to know."

"Do you think he'll ask?"

"I hope he does," Becca was surprised at her urgent response.

"So you'd say yes," Lydia smiled slyly.

"No, I'd say no," she playfully swatted at her mother, "of course I'd say yes. I can't live without him, you know that."

"Oh, my girl is growing up so fast," Lydia cooed, "when can I expect grandchildren?"

"Mom!" Becca hissed, "how about you focus on raising your own child before worrying about when I'm going to have mine. That's a long way away."

Lydia gave up without much of a fight and continued to watch the boys chase the nearly deflated soccer ball up and down the front yard.

Becca settled in against the step railing and let her mind float over the conversation she'd just finished.

School took a lot of Becca's attention. If there were lucid moments of free thought she often was busy updating or being updated by Emma or her mother, or immersing herself in Jamie's attention.

Daydreaming had not been atop her priority list. Perhaps she didn't need to daydream about a future marriage with Jamie. Perhaps she already knew that was where life would take her, and when the time came, she'd think of it all then.

But now, in the evening dimness and in the company of all that she loved, she let her mind wander away, past the front yard, past Colorado and far away to a life after college. To work, to a home. To greeting her husband, to raising children with him. To journeying through life next to him.

It was exhilarating, how assured she felt thinking over the future. She knew that she and Jamie would be together forever, would get married, raise a family and be innately happy. Becca was thrilled at what her future held. Whether anyone else knew it or not.

CHAPTER 13

"Jamie!" Becca cried out; a half whine, half alarmed shriek that echoed through their apartment.

With a small chuckle Jamie answered back, not moving from his seat on the sofa or lifting his eyes from the magazine he was leafing through.

Huffing, Becca stamped her right foot, "come here." The alarm in her earlier call to him gave way to a complete childlike whimper.

Jamie placed the magazine on the coffee table and strode the eight feet into the bathroom where Becca had been stationed for the last forty-five minutes.

She didn't turn, but glared at him in the mirror when he stood behind her.

"I can't get this damn zipper all the way up," she said to him, her voice deflated, her eyes wild.

The zipper on her dress was stuck on a millimeter of fabric.

Maneuvering it out of the way, he zipped her up tight and smiled in the mirror as he reached to the front of her neck and straightened the heart shaped pendant hanging from her necklace.

"You look like you're going to pass out," he said softly, patting the pendant then placing his hands on her shoulders and pulling her into him.

Exhaling loudly, he could feel her relax against him, "I'm sick to my stomach," she confessed, "they haven't paid a bit of attention for three years and all of a sudden it's 'we miss you' and 'we're coming to see you' oh my favorite 'we'll be there tomorrow'," she closed her eyes and leaned her head against his chest, "she's going to hate that I dyed my hair again."

"Of course she is," Jamie laughed, making Becca laugh with him, "my mother is going to hate everything,

Becca. Your hair, your dress, the apartment, our classes, the weather, the flight, the color of the carpet, everything."

"My dress?" Becca wailed with laughter, "I paid good money for this dress!"

Jamie shrugged, "She could buy you the dress and she'd hate it. It's how she is. If she suddenly decided against disliking you, I'd have a heart attack."

Becca nodded and smiled at their reflections.

Mrs. Enders' discord with Becca wasn't wavering or ceasing, even with time and distance. It was just understood.

"Please don't be nervous," Jamie pleaded, kissing the top of Becca's styled hair.

"I know," she agreed, "it's just been a while since I've seen them."

"I promise it'll be fine," Jamie hugged her tightly, "it could be worse, they could be staying with us."

"Oh God!" Becca threw her arms up and left the bathroom, "you're right, let's get this show on the road," she smiled at him and gathered her purse and shawl by the front door, "for the record, I don't think I could have them stay here," she explained, motioning around the apartment.

"Me either," Jamie agreed, "too close of quarters, my love. Someone wouldn't make it out alive," he joked, opening the front door and switching on the kitchen light.

Becca eased out the door and waited for Jamie to securely lock it, "You have no idea," she muttered and winked at him.

This had not been the first time in all her interactions with Jamie's mother that she contemplated just how far back into her skull could her eyes conceivably roll. She had tried to harbor a giggle when she counted, silently, that it had crossed her mind at least ten times in the last two hours.

"Jamie, this building smells like bleach," Mrs. Enders observed as they stood at their door as Jamie unlocked it.

"Mother, that's a good thing," he sighed, "means it's clean."

He stood aside and motioned for his mother and father to enter the apartment ahead of himself and Becca.

Making eye contact with Becca, he rolled his eyes and they both grinned wildly, both knowing, without exchanging a word, that they each were accumulating eye rolls.

"It's so small!" Mrs. Enders exclaimed nearly on cue, as Jamie shut the door and stood beside Becca in the kitchen.

In six steps she evaluated the apartment and lingered with her hands on her hips by the bar, "Your room at home is bigger than this entire thing!"

Jamie nodded, "You're right, but this is our home, at least for another year, and we love it," he nudged Becca's side, "Dad, can I get you a Scotch?"

"Oh, please," Mr. Enders said from the balcony. He'd been quiet most of the evening and had been moseying around while Mrs. Enders flailed about.

"Jamie!" she sucked in.

"What, Mother?" Jamie laughed as he poured two drinks, "one for Dad and one for my ragging alcoholic of a girlfriend," he joked, handing a glass to his father and sipping from the other, "I'm kidding, Mother, Becca doesn't drink."

"And you do?" she hissed.

"Carol, please," Mr. Enders said evenly, "it's a great place you have here, kids. Love that balcony."

"It's amazing. When we had all that snow a few weeks ago we couldn't even get the doors open," Jamie explained, leaning against the countertop. He reached for

Becca's hand and pulled her into him, holding her tightly around the shoulders.

Under his protective and loving hold, Becca calmed down immensely. She knew all of the insults that Carol would hurl, all the passing judgment, all of the snide, rude and hurtful remarks. But knowing the plan of attack never made it easier to endure.

Mrs. Enders silently seethed, standing next to the counter, eyeing everything in view, touching nothing. Becca, Jamie and Michael continued their conversation about the apartment, school and the climactic difference of Colorado and North Carolina.

With nearly a full twenty minutes of Mrs. Enders silence, she begrudgingly took a seat on the very edge of the sofa, crossed her arms in front of her and sighed heavily.

Becca could have sworn that she saw Michael give an eye roll before he cleared his throat and turned around, "It's getting late, Carol, are you all set?"

Mrs. Enders stood with urgency and stalked to the door, slinging her purse from her shoulder, "It was wonderful seeing you Jamie, we'll get together for lunch tomorrow. I'll call you in the morning," she nodded and smiled at him.

"Sounds great, Mother," he agreed, squeezing his hold on Becca.

"Goodnight," Becca smiled evenly. Carol hadn't said two words to her directly all evening.

"Goodnight, Becca," Mr. Enders came around the counter and hugged her, then Jamie, "Jamie. See you tomorrow kids."

"Night Dad," Jamie left Becca's side to shut the door behind them. He locked it and leaned against it, kicking off his shoes and sighing, "Good grief, could she be more terrible?" he untucked his shirt and came back to sit in one of the bar stools, "I swear to you, Becca, she has always been hard and I hate that she blatantly ignores you, but I just don't think I can fight her on it anymore."

Becca bit down on her bottom lip and leaned across the counter on her elbows, "I understand. We can't change her mind about me. I could save that woman's life and she'd still despise me. It doesn't matter though," she reached out and laced her fingers with Jamie's, "all that matters is you and me."

Jamie tiredly smiled, "That is why I love you. Not many people could take such undeserved treatment and smile beautifully afterward."

"Oh just wait. In thirty minutes I'll be crying and begging for her approval," Becca joked, unknotting her hands and slipping the pin from her hair. She yawned and kicked her heels off, letting them clunk against the bathroom wall, "I'm turning in," she smiled at Jamie, "will you help me with this zipper again?" she asked turning off the kitchen light and easing into their bedroom.

Jamie popped off the stool and followed her, "If I must," he sighed with sarcasm in his voice.

Becca turned on her heels and put her hands on his chest, "Oh, you don't have to. Don't want you to do anything you're not interested in. Just an offer," she shrugged, dropping her hands.

Jamie wrapped her in a tight hug, "Offer accepted," he said as they both laughed.

CHAPTER 14

"Can I ask you a personal question?"

Becca looked up from her seat on the floor beside the coffee table, "Okay," she smiled slowly.

"How can you concentrate with that going on?"

Kim Hager, a friend of Becca and Jamie's that shared their Business Communications class, asked Becca, with a wide eyed grin. The three of them were in the same project group deemed to create a business marketing packet for a faux software company.

Kim had been at the apartment all afternoon sifting through magazines and other possibilities trying to get their packet together.

Becca laughed and raised her eyebrows, "With what going on?" she asked.

Kim sucked in air as she blushed before lurching forward, "With him in there showering," she gulped, "with the door cracked open," she squealed, "he's beautiful, Becca. I'm so envious, it's disgusting."

Sensing Kim's innocent crush was something Becca had caught onto early in their assignment.

Becca snickered and looked back down at the picture she was cutting, "Oh, well sometimes is difficult. It's far worse when he walks around here naked. I can't get anything done," she sighed, looking up slowly at Kim who was now gawking, "but don't worry. He won't walk around here naked when we have company."

With as straight a face as Becca had ever seen on anyone, Kim asked, "Can you please ask him to?"

Finally cracking up, Becca threw a magazine in Kim's general direction, "No, I will not."

Giggling Kim went back to work. After a few minutes, when each heard the water stop running, the shower door open and close, they exchanged glances.

When Jamie emerged, fully clothed, his hair gelled, he sat beside Kim on the couch.

"Hey, Kim," he said sweetly, reaching for one of the magazines there were stacked on the coffee table, "How's it going?"

"Fine, thank you," she said smiling at him with a sly grin.

Jamie glared at her and then at Becca, "Do you tell her these walls are paper thin and you can hear every conversation being held in a five-mile radius?"

As Kim's jaw fell, Becca shrugged, "I forgot," she cleared her throat, "Kim, he probably heard everything that you said. Even your request for a naked walk by."

Kim's face was as red as her hair, "I'm so sorry, but you know," she threw up her hands, "you could have thrown a girl a bone," she joked, overcoming her embarrassment rather quickly. Kim may have been envious of Becca's relationship with Jamie, but Becca was envious of Kim's ability to let anything slide off her back. Becca had been that way in high school, but had since lost some of her thick skin.

"Changing the subject!" Kim announced, tossing her magazine a side and picking up another one, "how do you guys feel about it being your last year? Any immediate plans for when this is all over?"

Becca and Jamie exchanged quick smiles, "Nothing really set in stone. Probably move back home, get started on life. Find jobs, place to live," Becca shrugged.

"Get married, have kids," Jamie added enthusiastically.

"You guys are going to get married?" Kim asked, matching his enthusiasm.

"It hasn't been seriously discussed," Becca pipped up, "no one has been asked yet," she and Kim both glared at Jamie.

He leaned back, "We all know that's where we are headed. I'll ask when the time is right."

"Awe," Kim and Becca sighed together.

Becca may have been acting nonchalant, but she knew that look in Jamie's eyes, that smile on his face. He was serious. He was genuine. And she was elated.

CHAPTER 15

The room was bounding with energy. They had managed to fit fifteen people in a space hardly big enough for two. Jamie's birthday party was coming to an end, some of the guests had already left, some were working on a second piece of cake. Perched on the countertop in the kitchen, Becca eased in and out of the conversations being held around her. She was more interested in Jamie.

He had been corralled out onto the balcony with a handful of the guys and the door was left open. The cool February air would cascade into the small apartment, every now and then, reaching Becca and causing her to shiver.

She watched Jamie laugh at his friends' stories, at their jokes. His face gleaming, his features glowing with every word. Becca could feel herself mirror his expressions; if he smiled she did, if he raised his eyebrows, she did. Taking in everything about Jamie was one of her favorite things to do.

When he caught her gaze, he held it, smiling back just as wide or winking at her before returning to his friends.

Watching him across the room, with each breath feeling utterly giddy that he was hers. She still got butterflies when he was near, when he'd be on his way home, even after all the years they spent together.

Jamie seemed to be equally as enthralled. He greeted her any time it called for, with hugs or usually a kiss, be it when he got home or when they'd meet in class.

Jamie had been discussing their future nonstop as of late. Graduation was in three months. They were adults. Life was moving fast and Jamie was making plans.

They had decided to move back to Oakwood after Graduation. Jamie had a job prospect at the county newspaper. Becca missed her mother and Ben tremendously and had applied for a position at a new publishing firm that was opening up in Raleigh. Unbeknownst to Carol, Michael had been emailing them realtor information and local homes and apartments that were on the market.

Becca and Jamie had a plan in place: move home, get jobs, stay with Lydia until they got on their feet, and get married.

They had heard it from everyone, aside from Carol, about when they'd get married. Emma called every other day and her first questions was always "Has he asked yet?". Becca was surprisingly alright with the consistent bellyaching and the undefined reasons for Jamie's hesitance. She knew it would happen, Jamie had assured her. He had also assured her that he wanted certain things in place and to have a slight chance at surprising her. That was good enough for her.

As she absentmindedly thanked their guests and escorted them out, her mind drifted about the tentative plans they made for their future, the excitement that came with the knowing as well as the unknowing.

When the last guests said their goodbyes and Becca locked the door behind them, she was still in the euphoric haze of future happiness as Jamie, without a single word being said, gathered her in his arms and made her feel as if she could float there forever. Happy, safe and loved.

CHAPTER 16

Becca rapped her fingertips against the cars center console and raised her eyebrows challengingly in Jamie's direction, "Where are we going?" she asked smoothly, watching the line of trees pass behind Jamie's head as he drove.

He chuckled quickly and smiled, "Well, you know, Dad has been helping me out by checking out the market. When I talked to him last night he mentioned taking a look at one particular place that seemed to be in our price range. He emailed pictures and it looks promising."

"And you didn't show me?"

Jamie looked at her knowingly, "I wanted it to be a surprise," he said evenly, "I have a good feeling about this one."

"You've said that about a few," Becca pointed out with a sigh.

Jamie and Becca had been living with Lydia since moving back to Oakwood in June. Now October, it been a long four months. Jamie had got the job in the publishing office of the county paper and Becca was wrapping up an internship at Lashley Publishing, a new book firm in Raleigh that had opened over the summer.

"I know, but this one," Jamie took a deep breath and exhaled as he pulled into a driveway, stopping behind his father's car, "this one is different," he said confidently, turning off the car and smiling wickedly at her.

The house hunting process had been excruciating. Jamie had established credit and had been approved for financing for a home loan long ago. Finding a home that they agreed on was the hard part Jamie liked every house they came across. Becca wanted a home, a place she could see them spending a lifetime. She hadn't found that yet.

Becca laughed at Jamie's confidence and stepped out of the car, looking at the house. It was a beautiful, a two story sand stone house with white trim and black shutters, with a small front porch. The driveway was big enough to park two cards side by side, two deep.

"It's pretty," Becca conceded with a crooked smile. She really liked the outside.

"Good morning!" Mr. Enders called from the front porch. He waved and stepped down to the first step, "the realtor is a friend of mine, dropped off the keys this morning, said to help ourselves," his grin matched the one spread across Jamie's face.

"It looks nice from out here," Becca nodded, "Morning, Mr. Enders," she laughed and shook her head. If Carol had known Michael had been helping, she'd probably have a breakdown.

"Rebecca," he greeted, a tone of satisfaction and enthusiasm in his voice.

Mr. Enders unlocked the front door and walked in with a flourish, "Some rooms have been recently remodeled. It's unfurnished and pretty cheap for this area."

Becca whistled when she stepped in and took her first look around. The foyer was open. A half wall was on either side of the entry, the left of the front door had a wide top that could be used as a shelf. The right opened to view the kitchen.

The kitchen was big, but had been recently redone with green and black accents. A little dark for Becca's taste but the size of it was amazing. Along the front wall was counter space with windows facing the front yard, the countertop against the entire wall wrapped around to the adjacent wall as well, forming an L shape. Appliances tucked into the counters fit like a puzzle. The space had an island countertop in the middle and room enough for a dining room table.

Becca eased through the kitchen to the laundry room that was butted against the back of the house. The kitchen and the laundry room were probably bigger than their Colorado apartment combined.

She stood in the center of what would be the living room and spun in a circle slowly. There were two gigantic windows facing the front yard. A booming fireplace on the adjacent wall with built in bookshelves above it. The living room stretched to the back of the house where a set of French doors presumably extended to the back yard.

"What do you think so far?" Jamie asked, sneaking up behind her and squeezing her shoulders.

Becca nodded, "I'm impressed. Can we go upstairs?"

She didn't wait for Jamie or Michael to respond before sprinting upstairs. She was getting excited.

At the top of the stairs there was a balcony railing along the stairwell and wrapped around. To the right were three doors. One was a small guest room, a bathroom and what had to be the master bedroom with its own bathroom. To the left were two more doors, two more bedrooms.

Jamie followed her from room to room discussing details with his father. However, Becca heard very little of their conversation. Her brain was in a different mode. She was thinking of décor, where their few pieces of furniture from Colorado would go, what bedroom could be a nursery.

"Jamie," she said, her voice low as she stood in the first spare bedroom on the right of the stairs. Its windows were wide, facing the next door neighbor's yard, a closet reached the length of the wall. She heard him enter the room and turned to face him, "I think this is it," she smiled and grabbed his hand, "I have a good feeling here. I'm comfortable here."

"Yeah?" Jamie looked excited, "are you sure?" Because I'll have Dad make an offer right now."

Becca nodded, "What do you think?"

"I like it," he smiled so wide the corners of his eyes creased, "I knew when I saw it that was something about this house that felt right."

Becca glanced around again and nodded, "Yes, this is it. Make an offer," she smiled again.

Jamie took her hand and led them back down the stairs where his father was surveying the fireplace, "Tell Kevin we want to make an offer, Dad," Jamie smiled, "this is the one."

Mr. Enders looked pleased, "Alright, I'll get him on the phone. I'll let you know when I hear anything," he smiled, locked up the house behind them and waved as he pulled out his cell phone. They circled the block then parked back in front of the house.

"We're going to get it, I just know it," Becca gleamed, starting up at the house.

CHAPTER 17

"Do you think this house is too big?" Jamie asked with a sigh.

Becca laughed and rocked backward, "It's a bit too late, don't you think?"

He nodded, "Yeah, but," he looked around, "we have a four-bedroom house and own, what fifteen pieces of furniture? The scale is off."

"Well, sure, now it looks bare, but in time we'll fill it up. In ten years we could have seven kids and it'll be too small," she said promptly.

Jamie dove into the cardboard box laying in front of him that contained an artificial Christmas tree, "Is it bad that one of the fifteen pieces of furniture we own is a Christmas tree?" he asked flatly, pulling pieces from the box.

The had been in their new home on Gable Lane a little over three weeks. Christmas was a week away and they had finally gotten around to buying a tree and a few decorations.

The house did seem huge in comparison to the amount of things in it. Besides the appliances that come with the house, the living room set Jamie's father bought for them and the bedroom set of Becca's dreams her mother bought they had very little.

"I have a confession," Becca whistled as she laid out the Christmas ornaments they had bought. She watched Jamie lift his head and smile at her, "I know they just redid the kitchen, but we have to paint it or something. That green is too much."

It was Jamie's turn to rock back from his seated position on the floor, "Thank God you said it because I vomit a little every time I have to walk in there."

They laughed with agreement, "We can do this tonight, come on," Jamie shot up from the floor and straightened his outfit, "let's go get painting supplies. I'm doing that tomorrow," he said reaching for Becca and pulling her to her feet.

"Seriously?" she looked at him.

"Yes, seriously. What is not serious about vomit?" he kissed her cheek, "we've got all weekend to get it done, let's go," he said to her excitedly.

She followed him out the door, barely having enough time to grab her purse and slip her shoes on. Snow had begun to fall that afternoon and it lightly covered their front yard.

"I'll call mom. She and Ben can come help, either paint or do the tree and they could stay the night. Ben likes to camp in the spare room," Becca suggested, pulling her coat close to her to ward off the cold air.

"Sounds perfect," Jamie sloshed through the snow and ambled to the car, shivering while he started it and waited for the heat to kick in. He looked at her, sitting beside him and smiled, "I love you always," he said through chattering teeth.

Becca leaned over and kissed him sweetly, "What color should we paint?"

Jamie backed down the driveway and chuckled, "Any color that doesn't induce vomiting. I'll take pink at this point."

Becca settled into her seat, smiling at Jamie's sense of humor.

This was Jamie. Always happy, always ready to do the next project. Always moving. Always lively. Becca knew she was lucky. She knew that life was far different than it had been when she was a teenager. And she knew it was all because of Jamie.

CHAPTER 18

Becca laid sheepishly in their bed, her eyes barely open, her brain slowly waking up. She yawned and rolled over to face Jamie's side of the bed. Reaching out and smacking his pillow she sighed. She could hear the water beating against the stone tiles in their shower and she smiled. Pulling the covers up to her chest, she waited for it.

Glancing at the alarm clock, her smile widened as she heard the shower doors glide open.

"Becca, get up," she heard Jamie yell to her, "you're going to miss the entire day!"

Laughing she rolled onto her stomach. It never failed; every morning at 7:10 am Jamie would be up and in the shower, and if she weren't as well, he'd be calling her to wake up shortly after.

Closing her eyes, she eased back to sleep for a short few minutes and was jolted awake when she heard the shower door open and close again.

"I have a headache," she called out with a whine before he had a chance to repeat his prior announcement.

After a few minutes of silence, Jamie entered the room from their connecting bathroom, pulling a shirt over his head then buckling his belt, "You didn't even drink that much," he teased her, running his fingers through his hair and standing at the foot of the bed, "light weight."

Becca creased her eyebrows, "Am not," she pouted.

Jamie grabbed a handful of comforter, "Alright," he gave in, "come on, get up. We have a busy day."

"I didn't know we had anything planned."

"Well, we do," Jamie smiled, "I'm going to cook breakfast," he let go of the bedding and came around the side to kiss Becca, "get up," he said with a smile as he left the room.

With the enthusiasm and pace of a slug, Becca poured herself out of bed, into the shower and into some clothes before slumping downstairs. The hot shower and two Advil's were beginning to alleviate her headache. She grumbled to herself as she entered the kitchen looking for Jamie, "Aren't you supposed to sleep in on New Year's Day? You know, sleep it off, whatever insane thing you did at whatever New Year's Eve party you went to?"

Becca sighed, finding Jamie sitting outside on the porch swing. She sat beside him and he handed her a plate. The snow was melting and the sunshine felt good on her back.

"Greasy food is supposed to help a hang over," he shrugged. There was a fried egg and bacon bagel sandwich on her plate, "or so I've heard," he said taking a bite of his own sandwich, "besides," he chewed and swallowed and raised his eyebrows, "New Year's Eve party? You had three Margaritas at your mother's house. Doesn't qualify."

"I don't know if I can eat this," Becca shook her head, an embarrassed smile on her face.

"If you don't, Mrs. Nye will," Jamie motioned across the street, "she's been eyeing it since I came out here."

"June?" Becca laughed and slyly looked across the street to see June Nye not so bashfully watching them, "she doesn't want breakfast, she wants you," Becca giggled, nudging Jamie in the ribs.

He shivered and bit his bottom lip, "That's just inappropriate. She's so old," he whispered.

Laughing as she took her first bite, Becca covered her mouth, "In case you haven't noticed, everyone in this neighborhood is old."

They ate their breakfast quietly for a few minutes.

"So what's the plan for today?" Becca asked, sipping some of the orange juice he had handed her.

"The new furniture place in Durham is having some big holiday sale. I wanted to see about finding a coffee table that matched the sofa and chair maybe," he smiled at her.

Becca widened her glare, "Who told you about that?"

Jamie shrugged, "Mark had mentioned at work the other day. Grant had said he got a lot of stuff discounted on opening day," he explained.

Finishing their breakfast and getting themselves ready for the day, they settled in to the car for the hour trip east.

Becca was laughing at Jamie who was happily singing along to the songs on the radio, but kept singing the wrong lines, thinking he knew which line would be next.

"You should just stop, really," Becca laughed as she fished through her purse searching for her cell phone that was ringing.

"Hello?" she said, laughter still in her voice.

"Bonjour!" Emma's voice rang out clearly.

"Bonjour to you, Mrs. Sherver," Becca squealed, "it's so odd saying that."

"I know, right?" Emma agreed, "how was your new year's?"

"Not as exciting as yours I bet," Becca focused her attention out the window.

Emma chuckled, "Oh, Becca don't be sad," she shushed.

Emma had called the prior morning explaining that she and Remi had decided to elope on New Year's Eve. No warning, no wedding, no planning. Just do it. And they did.

"I'm elated for you," Becca said through clenched teeth, "I just wish I had been there. I'm jealous."

"I wish you were here too, but it was just so sudden," she paused, "you have to swear that I'm your first call when Jamie pops the question."

Becca rolled her eyes, "If that ever happens," she said with slight disgust. They hadn't brought up marriage in a while. In the past Becca had been fine with waiting for Jamie's "perfect" scenario, but now it seemed that the waiting was becoming evasive.

"It will, I know it," Emma reassured her, "so what are you up to today?"

They continued talking until Jamie parked in front of the store. Becca nodded absently, trying to tell Emma goodbye and giggled to herself as Jamie sat next to her, smacking his lips together, making a Tisk noise each time. This was something he did whenever he was nervous or bored.

Finally hanging up, she sighed and exited the car, "Emma says hello and to tell you that married life is amazing," she dramatized the last part and slammed her door shut, stalking into the store. She was highly on edge today, and not sure why, possibly the lingering bits of headache.

Making quick work of the store and finding the coffee table Jamie had wanted, they squeezed it into the car and headed back home.

The ride had been fairly silent, which Becca found herself grateful for.

"I think I'm going to take a nap," she said as they sat the table down in the living room and looked at her watch, "it's not even noon yet and I'm feeling pretty crappy. Did you have anything else planned?

Jamie looked hesitant and then shook his head, "Not until later," he waved this hand toward the stairs, "but go, get some rest," he smiled and leaned into her, kissing her gently, "love you."

"Always," she smiled and trudged up the stairs. She found two more Advil and swallowed them with a gulp of water and snuggled back into bed. She was fast asleep within minutes.

When she woke up, hours later, she felt calmer and the throbbing pain picking in her head had subsided.

Checking the alarm clock, she sighed. It was nearly three o'clock. She had slept the day away.

Stretching she climbed out of bed, went to the bathroom and brushed her hair.

The house was silent as she descended the stairs, but saw Jamie sitting on the couch with his lap top, his feet on the new coffee table.

"Hi," she said sleepily, stepping over his legs and sitting beside him.

"So, Sleeping Beauty is awake," he joked, "feeling better?" he asked closing his computer.

She nodded, "Much. Thank you for letting me sleep."

Jamie smiled and placed the computer on the table, "Henry called. He said they have two manuscripts for you to pick up Monday."

"Goody, more work," Becca sunk in beside him, "I hope they aren't as tedious as the last two."

"Editing is tedious by nature," he sighed.

Nodding slowly Becca sighed, "So what else did you have planned for today or did I sleep through it all?" she asked rubbing her eyes.

Jamie was quiet, leaning against her as well and took a deep breath, "No other real plans, but uh," he paused, "I did want to show you something."

She didn't budge, "What is it?"

"Just an idea I had," he stood up and pulled her with him, leading her to the kitchen, "now, uh," he paused again, smacking his lips, "stand over here, from this angle," he led her across the kitchen to stand next to the sink, "what do you think?"

"About what?" she questioned with a laugh.

"About the island in relationship to the table," he said, booming, "should we move them?"

Becca caught a laugh in her throat, "If you think I'm demolishing this island, you're nuts."

"Okay," Jamie started slowly, "but look over here, I just think it's crowded," he said, taking her hand and leading her to the other corner of the kitchen, "now look."

She was standing in the far corner of the kitchen, her back to the laundry room, next to the table. She couldn't see a difference. Nothing he was saying made sense. The thought of tile dust and concreate made her sick, "What am I looking at now?" she asked, laughing clearly.

"This," he answered.

In a movement so quick that Becca wasn't sure how it happened, Jamie was standing directly behind her. She could feel his chest on her back and he was reaching around her, his hand out in front of her. A diamond ring between his fingertips.

She gasped so loudly that she clamped her hand over her mouth and started shaking.

With the other hand Jamie gripped her arm, "Rebecca, I love you more than any words could express. I've wanted to do this for a very long time, but I wanted you to be thoroughly surprised," he whispered in her ear, still standing behind her, "please, Becca, will you marry me?"

At the sounds of the words Becca had dreamed about for years, she cried. She was crying so hard she couldn't answer immediately. After a few deep breaths, she screamed, "Yes!" and shuddered against Jamie's body.

He kissed her cheek as he slipped the classic, three stone diamond ring onto her finger and turned her around in his arms.

She clasped him in a hug and began kissing him excitedly.

She couldn't believe it. Finally!

"Jamie, it's gorgeous," she cried out between kissed, "how, when, why?"

Separating for explanation Jamie was just as excited as she was, "It's stunning, right?" they laughed, "only the best for you," he brushed pieces of her hair behind her ears and smiled, "I have been saving for a while and when I saw it, I knew it was the one. I've had it for a few weeks, just waiting for the right moment. I had decided to ask last night at your moms, but Emma blew that plan up," he laughed again, "but I couldn't wait anymore," he wiped her tears, "I'm sorry I took so long!"

"It was perfect, absolutely perfect," she hurriedly hugged him again, "I'm so happy!"

The stood clenched in each other's arms before the excitement exploded.

"We have to tell mom," Becca screeched, "we have to go over there, I have to see her face!" she let go of him and started pulling her boots and coat on.

Jamie agreed and they raced to the car. Jamie intertwined her fingers with his while he drove, both of them gazing at the ring.

Becca couldn't take her eyes off of it. It was gorgeous. It was too beautiful for words. He had done such a great job, catching her off guard with his proposal. Although she knew it would happen and she had been dreaming about it, she didn't think he was anywhere near ready yet. He sure fooled her.

Pulling into her mother's driveway, Becca nearly exploded out of the car before Jamie had it stopped. Waiting less than five seconds for him to get out was excruciating; she was bursting with happiness.

She grabbed his hand and sprinted toward the house, up the snow covered stairs and bolted through the front door like they were on fire.

"Mom!" Becca screamed with a delight and volume she hadn't used in a while.

Halting in the center of the hallway, her mother and Ben meeting them as they ran from the kitchen. Lydia had no chance to ask what was going on.

"We're getting married!" Becca screeched, thrusting her hand at her mother, who looked shocked.

The room was silent for a split moment before howling and more crying broke out.

"Oh, sweet heavens, I can't believe it!" Lydia screamed, taking her daughters hand to look at the ring, "in all that is Holy, that is magnificent!" she hugged Becca tightly and moved toward Jamie, "come here, you," she cried hugging him, "oh, I love you!"

"It's about time," Ben smiled, his braces gleaming, "congratulations," he gave his sister a half hug.

"I think I'm in shock," Lydia laughed, clapping her hands together.

"You?" Becca laughed, "I've got shocked covered."

"It's just," Lydia paused, overwrought with emotion, "it's wonderful, it really is. You two belong together, oh," she shook her head, "we have to start planning. We have to pick a date, we have to have an engagement party," she threw her hands up.

They scattered around the small kitchen table with notepads and pens, heaving out ideas well into the evening. Becca stayed close to Jamie, smiling at him, and taking in each moment.

This was amazing, a moment she wanted to remember forever. The energy, the happiness, the excitement.

Emma couldn't contain herself when Becca called to tell her. She was thrilled and shocked that Jamie hadn't mentioned a word of his plans to her.

By nightfall the had planned and booked their engagement party to be in two weeks and had a list of possible wedding dates.

Jamie was just as enthusiastic as Becca was, much to her pleasing. She couldn't imagine having him be anything less than ecstatic.

This was the beginning of their life together. This was the beginning of the rest of their lives with each other.

CHAPTER 19

Becca sipped her wine, while shaking her head. She reached up and brushed her bangs to the side of her face as she pointed her glass at Emma and Remi who were sitting across the table from her and Jamie.

"I could do it and you know I could," she defended, raising her eyebrows at Emma who was now laughing

"There is no doubt in my mind, Becca, that you are strong, but that's a pain neither of us know," she pointed out, sitting back in her seat, "what do you think Mrs. McKenon?"

Lydia finished the last bite of her slice of cheesecake and sighed deeply, "I think if you put your mind to it, you can do whatever you want. Pain or no pain," she agreed with her daughter, "however, there is nothing wrong with having a little help. It is simply excruciating," she shuddered at the memory.

Becca turned her gaze toward Jamie and licked her lips in victory, "I'll show you," she nodded, "every one of our children will be delivered without any drugs. Watch me," she said proudly.

"What if we end up with sextuplets or you're medically unable to deliver naturally?" Jamie pointed out to her.

She wasn't giving in, "Nope, I'll do it. Just to prove you wrong."

Jamie smirked and kissed her forehead, "Okay. But the instant you break, I'll be there, just smiling with total satisfaction," he prodded.

Lydia cleared her throat, "As entertaining as this conversation has been, I don't think it's something to wager on, the birth of your children."

As the table laughed together, Remi asked in broken English, "When will you start a family?"

"As soon as possible," Jamie answered at the same time Becca said, "We have time."

They looked at each other and exchanged sweet smiles.

Jamie had been nonstop as of late with his discussion and interest in starting a family. Becca found it wonderful that he was so ready to begin that chapter, however she was still reeling from the stress of planning the wedding.

"Well," Lydia announced, breaking into Becca's thoughts, "As amazing and graphically informative this evening has been," she tousled Ben's hair, "I think it's time we head out. After all, we each have a big day tomorrow," she grinned wildly.

After paying the bill, they congregated outside; Lydia and Ben waiting to whisk Becca away to traditionally spend the evening apart from her soon to be husband. Jamie, Emma and Remi were heading back to the house to handle any last minute preparations. Emma and Remi were staying at Becca and Jamie's while they were in town.

"Are you sure you have everything that you need from the house? You're completely packed for the wedding and set to leave immediately afterward?" Jamie checked once more before they said goodnight.

It had been extremely hectic for Becca, finishing up her packing that morning, but she felt she had all she'd need.

She nodded and wrapped her arms around him, "It'll be fine," she rested her forehead against his.

"I can't believe tomorrow we'll be married," he sighed happily, reaching his arms around her and rubbing her back.

"I can't believe tomorrow at this time we'll be dreaming in Savannah," she breathed, "a simple, quiet, peaceful Honeymoon."

"Peaceful," he echoed, "just what we need."

Becca tightened her grip, "I can't wait."

"To marry me or to be on vacation?" Jamie asked jokingly.

"Both," she smiled at him and kissed him softly, "but to marry you wins by a pinch."

They stayed in each other's arms for a while longer until their respective company started to complain. They said their goodbyes and parted ways.

Becca was quiet in her mother's car, watching out the window as Oakwood passed her by. She couldn't describe what she was feeling, but she never wanted it to go away. She was floating, full of happiness that tonight she's be Rebecca McKenon and tomorrow she'd be Rebecca Enders. Jamie's wife. The love of his life. She honestly didn't know how she was going to be able to wait until tomorrow.

CHAPTER 20

Becca had her picture taken so much in the last ten minutes all she could see were dots. Blinking rapidly, she laughed and tried to smile.

"Enough, please," she announced, holding her hands up while she closed her eyes, "I can't see a damn thing," she exhaled with a laugh.

Emma chuckled, "Sorry," she placed her camera on the table beside her, "you look beautiful."

"Thank you," Becca sighed, trying to focus on the dots disappearing.

"Okay, girl," Lydia sashayed back into the room, "we have to get this veil on and then, I think," she paused and placed some Bobbie pins between her lips, "we're done."

Becca sat gingerly, careful not to make too many creases in her wedding gown. Her A-line, lace covered gown felt delicate and romantic. Lydia easily placed the veil atop her perfectly curled hair and pinned it into place.

"Done," Lydia said quietly, stepping back.

"Oh," Emma gasped and grabbed for the camera.

"No, no more picture right now, please," Becca laughed. She got up and looked at her reflection in the mirror, "oh my," she smiled, "this is really happening."

Emma squealed with excitement and clapped her hands together, "Finally," she hugged her best friend.

Becca was taking deep breaths when someone knocked on the door.

"Who is it?" Lydia questioned.

"Uh," the voice stuttered, "Kim. Ben told me Becca was in here?"

"Oh, Kim!" Becca screamed and flung open the door.

The girls exchanged hugs and various excited greetings.

"I'm so glad you could make it! Kim, this is my mom and my best friend Emma," she introduced.

Kim extended her hand and smiled at Lydia and Emma, "So nice to finally meet you," she turned back to Becca, "of course I'd come to this! Being around you two turned me into a hopeless romantic," she laughed, "Becca, the church is gorgeous and Jamie looks amazing."

"I haven't seen him," Becca blushed. She had been quite positive he'd look stunning in his classic cut black suit, but it always felt good to have validation from an outside source.

Kim nodded, "Well, I know things are about to get started, but I wanted to say a quick hello. I will catch up with you later," Kim hugged Becca tightly and vanished out the door in a wave of red silk.

Becca turned back to her mother and her matron of honor and exhaled nervously, "I suddenly feel sick," she confessed, holding her stomach.

"I'm so excited, I think I'm going to burst." Emma's voice pitched and they giggled, "I'll go check, see how things are going out there."

Leaving Becca and Lydia alone for a moment, Lydia beamed, "I'm so proud of you, girl. You are so beautiful and you're marrying your true love, it's special."

Becca dabbed away a stray tear and smiled, "Do you think Carol said that to Jamie?"

Lydia shook her head, still with a smile, "No, girl. She probably attempted to talk him out of it. But she's evil, so it's okay," she winked at her daughter.

The Enders had very little to do with anything related to the wedding. Michael had given Jamie some money to cover a few of the expenses, however, Carol had a negative amount of interest. It was rather shocking to even see that she had shown up at the Church that morning. Becca, quiet honestly, had prepared for some kind of fight to occur that day. Regardless of Carol's poor attitude, nothing was going to stop the most amazing moment of Becca's life.

Emma cracked the door open and stuck her head inside, "Everyone is here, seated and ready," the pitch of her voice made Becca giggle, "you ready?"

"I think so," Becca was nervous, shaking terribly.

Lydia grabbed her hand, "Come on, girl," she handed Becca her bouquet as Emma grabbed hers quickly.

They slowly walked out of the dressing area and to the closed doors of where the wedding ceremony would be held. Through small windows, Becca could see the crowd, their friends and family. It wasn't a big crowd, they knew few people, but enough. She spotted Ben, sitting in the front row. His black and white tux was bothering him; he was picking at the neck.

She forced herself to skip looking at Jamie, standing at the altar. She wanted her first sight of him to be as she was walking toward him. She grinned, eyeing Grant, Jamie's best man, standing nervously. She hoped he'd be alright. He was an editor at the newspaper and wasn't good with crowds, more a behind the scenes guy.

"Last chance," Emma winked at her.

"No way," Becca smiled, gulping back tears that suddenly sprang to her eyes, "go," she laughed.

Emma opened the small doors. After one last look back with a smile, she made her way slowly down the aisle.

Lydia looped her arm through Becca's and clasped her hand, "You ready?" she asked again, pride in her voice.

Becca nodded, "I'm going to cry."

"That's what you're supposed to do, girl," Lydia patted Becca's arm.

When her music began to play, Becca took a final deep breath and began her walk down the aisle, her mother proudly beside her.

Sweet gasps rang out and some whispers, but Becca's attention was focused on Jamie.

She felt Lydia tighten her grasp as she beamed at Jamie.

He was stunning. Standing at the altar, smiling widely, hands knotted, suit perfect. He was her angel, her everything.

His grin never wavered as she kept eye contact with him until she was in front of him.

The ceremony began and Becca went through the motions, hugging her mother tightly after she had given her away to be married, and handing her bouquet over to a sobbing Emma.

When she intertwined her hands with Jamie and faced him, her nerves vanished. She was at ease, comforted by Jamie's presence.

They said a prayer, exchanged their vows and rings, and kissed passionately when they had been announced as husband and wife.

The small room thundered with cheers and claps as they preceded down the aisle to the back of the church.

Their guests flanked the wide concrete stairs that led out to the waiting limo to escort them to the reception hall.

Becca took a deep breath of cool autumn air and watched in slow motion as leaves fell along with the flower petals their guests were tossing over their heads.

She was jolted back to reality when Jamie pulled their clenched hands toward him and kissed her, "I love you always," he said as they parted.

In the quiet of the limo, Becca brushed leaves and petals from her hair and grabbed Jamie tightly as if he were disappearing from her reach, "I can't believe we're married, my God you look gorgeous," she said breathlessly, kissing him.

"You're beautiful," Jamie said through a laugh. He reached up and caressed her face in his hands, "I can't tell you how happy you've made me, Mrs. Enders."

"Mrs. Enders," Becca repeated, "Becca Enders," she squealed loudly and shook her head, reminded of Emma's piercing squeals that morning.

Becca couldn't believe the amazement she felt all day long. This was her wedding day, she had married the man of her dreams, the man she was meant to spend her life with.

She floated around the reception, hand in hand with Jamie, greeting guests and posing for photographs. She was in a state of elation and was confident Jamie felt the same way. He hadn't let her go since she arrived at the altar.

When the DJ announced their first dance, Becca led Jamie to the center of the dance floor and melted into his embrace, singing along to the lyrics of the song. She was the happiest she had ever been and looked forward to her life with him.

When the song ended and the audience clapped, Jamie kissed her sweetly, "I love you always," he whispered to her intensely.

The remainder of the reception flashed by too quickly. They were hugging people goodbye and crying as Emma held Becca tightly. Becca and Jamie were leaving in the morning for their Honeymoon and Emma and Remi were flying back to Paris. Becca had missed having her best friend around the past few years.

"You have a better best friend now," Emma, teary-eyed, said to Becca, pushing her hair over her shoulders, "one to be beside you every day. I love you, but I've been replaced."

"Oh Emma!" Becca cried out, grasping her friend.

They said goodbye to their remaining friends and family. Becca thanked her mother for helping with absolutely everything and for walking her down the aisle. She grabbed Ben for a quick hug before he had the chance to escape.

They said a quick goodbye to Jamie's parents, who had, to Becca's disbelief, stayed for the entire reception.

The limo took them and their luggage to the hotel in Raleigh.

"Hello," Becca greeted the bewildered concierge at the lobby desk. She must have looked odd, in her white, lace wedding dress, rolling luggage behind her. Jamie checked them in, got their room key and led the way to the elevator.

Leaning against the wall, he exhaled loudly and smiled, "What a day, huh?" he laughing, rolling his head to look at her.

She nodded in agreement, closing her eyes, "I'll have to text mom about picking up the dress and suit tomorrow. Forgot to remind her."

"I'm sure she's got it covered," he laughed and shook his head, "I have to say, the sight of you in that dress in this dingy elevator is just the slightest bit amusing."

"I guess I'm over dressed," she joked, shrugging her shoulders as the elevator stopped and the doors opened.

She followed Jamie down the quiet hallway and to their room. A standard hotel room, quiet and dark. It wasn't home and that's all that mattered. She wanted to spend their wedding night away from any reminders of stress.

Jamie stacked the luggage together and loosened his neck tie, "So, Mrs. Enders," he smiled at her and took off his suit jacket, draping it across the chair, "what would you like to do now?"

Becca took a deep breath, "Well," she kicked off her shoes as did Jamie, "Mr. Enders," she slipped a few of the pins that were in her hair out and tossed them onto the bureau, "as much as I love this dress and I feel like a princess in it, I'm dying to get out of it."

Jamie looked blank for a moment, obviously not quite expecting her to get to the point with her answer, "Would you like some help with that?" he laughed.

She turned her back on him and pulled her hair over her shoulder, "Unzip me, but I warn you, Emma had a hell of a time getting me in this thing."

Still chuckling, Jamie confidently started unzipping slowly, "I think I may have a little more incentive," he kissed her exposed shoulder as she playfully swatted at him.

After a few seconds of tugging and fighting, Jamie laughed loudly, "This thing hates me."

Becca laughed with him, "I told you! There is something wrong with the zipper and I didn't have time to have it fixed."

Every few centimeters it would snag, causing Jamie to have to pull it back up then back down, making it move just a bit further then where he had begun.

"Can I just rip it? I mean, you're never going to wear it again and I seriously think I could just rip it off right now," he said, straining his voice.

"No!" Becca laughed hysterically, "just take your time," she sighed, and turned slightly to look at him, "we have the rest of our lives."

CHAPTER 21

Aimlessly wandering around their living room, Becca smiled at the framed wedding photo on the mantel above the fireplace. The memories of their wedding day came flooding back and she barely could believe they had been married three years. An even bigger amazement, Becca and Jamie had been together ten years.

Ten years since those days of high school.

She grabbed the wedding album off the shelf next to the fireplace, like she had a million times before, and sat down on the couch, opening it to a random page.

Their wedding album held fond memories. For Becca, it had been the best day of her life, marrying Jamie, becoming his wife. But the memories captured in these photos were also painful reminders of how the tides of life changed with time.

Neither she nor Jamie had spoken with Kim much over the last three years, but that wasn't unusual, they'd barely kept in touch between graduation and the wedding. The most painful was Emma. After the wedding, Emma and Remi returned to Paris and began their lives together. Before long they had moved to England and both were teaching at Cambridge. They had become world travelers while doing their work as researchers for the school. Contact was minimal, but within the last year it ceased completely.

Becca missed her best friend terribly and in turn had her life fully revolved around Jamie, her mother and Ben.

"Okay," Jamie said triumphantly, coming down the stairs to the living room, breaking through Becca's cloud of dismay, "I have successfully created a contraption with paper and tape that I don't think a bomb could break through," he smiled proudly and handed Becca the present he had worked so feverishly to wrap.

She looked it over and laughed, "it's going to take me until New Years to get this open."

His grin widened, "I know," he sat down beside her and took the album from her lap and sat it on the coffee table, "that was my plan. Go ahead, try and open it."

"It's isn't Christmas yet," Becca objected.

Glancing at his watch, Jamie said, "it'll officially be Christmas by the time you get the damn thing open," he giggled, shaking his head.

Taking a deep breath, Becca began to unwind the half roll of Scotch Tape he had used to keep the classic Santa Clause themed wrapping paper formed to the box no bigger than a compact disc case.

Jamie announced that it was midnight, officially Christmas, before she had even reached the actual paper.

Feeling like it would now be okay to open her gift, she dug her nails and ripped with joy.

She wadded up the paper and tape into a tight ball and chuck it at Jamie playfully. He caught it and smiled, "I'm keeping this," he said, raising his eyebrows.

"It's a beautiful box!" Becca exclaimed, rubbing her hand over the blue leather box with a laugh.

Jamie smirked, "I thought you'd love it," he said dramatically with a shy grin, "I mean, I knew that you were getting me the exact fishing gear that I have been pining over for two months now, by the way, love you for letting me try it out in the morning, so I knew that I had to get you something equally as wonderful. When I saw that box," he bit his bottom lip and shook his head, "I knew it was the one."

Hysterical at Jamie's over dramatic irrelevance, Becca popped the cover open on the box. Inside was a simple, braided gold chain.

"It's beautiful Jamie," she breathed, slipping it form the box, "can I wear it now?"

"Of course you can," Jamie took it from her and clasped it around her neck.

She straightened it and patted it on her chest. It fell lower than most the necklaces she had, hanging just above her shirt line.

"I love it, thank you," she leaned forward and kissed him, "Merry Christmas."

"Merry Christmas," he smiled at her happily.

CHAPTER 22

The soft morning light crept slowly through the open blinds and paneled curtains beyond the headboard of their bed.

"It's getting light out," Becca said gently, sing-song like.

Jamie groaned something inaudible and rolled from his side facing her to his stomach.

Giggling, Becca stretched and feathered his exposed back with her nails, "It's the last day of work before our mini vacation," she reminded him, slight excitement in her voice.

He moaned and groaned for another few minutes before begrudgingly rolling out of bed and into the shower.

Becca laid in bed for a few quiet moments, her eyes closed peacefully. She stretched, the soft sheets spreading over her bare body. Yawning, she quickly followed Jamie into the shower.

She felt a need to be near him this morning. Perhaps it was the way they had spent the early morning hours, so close to each other, that made her long to be in Jamie's presence. She begged him to call in sick for work and to leave early for their trip to the coast. He had considered it, but had a deadline for a project set.

Without much care, Jamie took his time getting ready for work that morning. Becca was clinging and he was feeling equally as drawn to her. He thought it was just one of those electric days. Running out the door late, they exchanged hurried plans to meet for lunch.

Becca spent most of the morning planning and packing for their weekend retreat to the coast. She had both their suitcases out and open on the bed, placing items into them carefully and mentally checking them off as she went. Jamie had trusted her to do all of his packing. She knew what he'd wear, what he wouldn't and what he needed.

Plus, they both agreed that it would save time; letting them leave first thing the next morning.

Nearing lunchtime, Becca gathered the two manuscripts she had finished the night before to drop them off to Henry on her way to meet Jamie. She had some light shopping to do for the trip as well and hoped she could get it all done before meeting Jamie.

The publishing office was quite a way from Jamie's building, so she drove quickly, maneuvering with caution to get to her destinations. Luckily, talkative Henry had left for lunch, so Becca left the manuscripts on his desk with a note and picked up the one that was waiting for her. He knew of Becca and Jamie's vacation so he gave her plenty of clearance for the deadline; three weeks.

She stopped at the closest market to Jamie's building and raced down the aisles. Tossing the bags in her back seat, she shook her head, frustrated that she was late.

She felt rushed and uneasy as she made her way to Jamie. She parked in an empty parallel spot, clocked the meter for two hours and bolted for his office on the fifth floor. She politely said hello to the people she passed and welcomed the sudden alleviation from the uneasiness she felt when she darted into Jamie's office.

He was on the phone. He smiled at her and gave a small wave before wrapping up the telephone call with an eye roll.

"Hey," he said with a sigh, popping up out of his chair and coming around the desk to kiss Becca.

"Hi," she said breathlessly.

"Are you ready?" he asked her, grabbing his cell phone and wallet from his desk, "I thought we could go to that deli around the corner," he suggested, taking her hand and leading her out.

"Sounds perfect," she hadn't realized until then that she hadn't yet eaten. She was famished, "how's your day coming so far?"

Jamie exhaled loudly as they entered the elevator, "A total mess," he mashed the lobby button on the panel, "Grant and I have that deadline today and the article mark that was being worked on got kicked back to me and has to be done today," he rolled his eyes again and smiled at her crookedly, "I may be late tonight."

She nodded, "That's alright. I have a new copy to do, it'll keep me busy, I finished packing already."

He laughed, "I can't wait to get out of this place," he confessed, exiting the elevator and weaving them through the lobby and onto the front sidewalk.

The August air had a slight hint of coolness to it, which made it comfortable outside. Becca felt complete ease once they reached the deli. Avoiding the immense line at the take out counter, Jamie led her to an empty booth toward the opposite end of the dining room. She slid into the booth next to Jamie and sighed heavily.

Their lunch date went quickly and before she knew it, they were saying goodbye in front of Jamie's building.

Becca reached up and clasped her hands behind Jamie's head, pulling him deeper into her kiss. Normally he was cautionary with public displays of affection, but this afternoon he returned her passionate kiss with alarming need.

They were breathless when they parted, and smiling.

"I wish I could leave now," Jamie said, biting his bottom lip, dread filling his face.

Becca didn't want to make him feel any worse so she shrugged, "You'll be done soon enough," she hugged him tightly and kissed him once more, gingerly, "I love you."

"I love you always," he replied, letting her go from his grasp but winking at her.

Walking away, she turned back to glance over her shoulder at Jamie, smiled at him and gave a quick wave. He waved back and she watched him disappear into the lobby.

The rest of the day she spent in a content splendor. She has already finished all the packing and decided to clean the house. At dinner time, she called Jamie to see how much longer he'd be.

"Hours," he sighed annoyingly, "they'll be lucky if I don't quit after this," he finished by telling her he loved her and that he'd be home as soon as possible.

Becca had dinner with her mother and Ben and spent the evening enjoying their company.

It was getting late when she returned home, Jamie's car still not in the driveway.

At ten o'clock Becca dialed Jamie's cell phone again and waited three rings.

"I am in the car," he laughed obviously knowing it was her, "let's leave tonight. We can sleep in the morning, I'll drive," he said to her excitedly with laughter.

It wouldn't take much to make her agreeable.

"It'll be ready when you get here. Love you," she smiled into the phone.

"I love you always," he said to her, his voice clearly joyous.

Becca pulled their bags downstairs and placed them close to the front door. She wanted to leave immediately.

Even with the excitement pulsing through her veins, she felt sleepy. Knowing Jamie would be home in less than an hour, she folded herself onto the couch, under an old blanket and fell asleep quickly, listening to a silent house and a light rain padding against the windows.

CHAPTER 23

The ringing of the telephone that she had placed near her pillow before she fell asleep jolted her so harshly, she instantly sat up to answer it.

"Hello?" she barked, her voice groggy, her limbs asleep.

"Mrs. Enders?" the voice was unfamiliar.

"This is she," she blinked hard and focused on her watch in the near pitch black of the house; two-forty-seven am.

Simultaneously she wondered where Jamie was as the caller continued to talk, "Mrs. Enders, this is Ronald Mays, from the Sery County Police Department. Is your husband Mr. James Michael Enders?"

Jamie. She looked around feverishly, "Yes, Sir. Where is Jamie?"

"Mrs. Enders there was an accident this evening involving your husband and another vehicle – "

"Where is he?" she interrupted, panic starting to well up in her stomach.

"He was transported to Cypress Regional Hospital, ma'am. It'll be in your best interest to come down here," he continued coolly.

"Is he alright?" she squeaked.

"The attendant in Emergency will be able to answer your questions, Mrs. Enders. I don't know the status of your husband." He hung up so suddenly, so coldly, that Becca threw the phone across the room. She sat reeling from what she had been told, her eyes darting about the dark room. Within seconds she bolted out the door, grabbing her purse.

She was scared. Her mind was all over the place with worry. What had happened? They had talked at ten o'clock, he was on his way home, everything was fine.

What could have happened? She kept thinking he'd be so angry at himself for causing her to worry so.

Suddenly feeling lost as she sped in the direction of the hospital, she fished through her purse for her cell phone. With shaking hands, she found it and called her mother.

"I'm sorry to wake you, but I need you at Cypress Hospital. It's Jamie," Becca said with surprising calmness.

Lydia didn't ask any questions. Even with the veil of calmness Lydia could sense the desperate terror. "I'll be there in ten minutes."

The phone slid easily from her hand back into her bag without conscious. She knew she'd be getting no other calls.

Becca tried to focus on the road, on the lines, on the lights of oncoming traffic. She tried to keep her mind blank, free of any thought of worry or the possibility of worse.

Reaching the hospital, she parked her car with a rush of relief and groan of despair as she ran into Emergency. Her gut wasn't feeling well.

Rushing to the nurse seated behind a long desk, Becca blurted, "I'm Becca Enders. My husband, Jamie, James Enders is here. Someone from the police department called me. He was in an accident."

"Have a seat ma'am, I'll check for you," the disheveled nurse slowly heaved herself out of her swivel chair and disappeared through a set of swinging double doors.

Becca looked around for an empty seat and collapsed in the closest one to the desk. She closed her eyes and steadied her breathing. She felt nervous, scared. Her skin was crawling.

After a few minutes the same nurse stuck her head out of the heavy doors, "Is anyone here with you, ma'am?" she asked, creasing her forehead.

Becca felt confused. She shook her head, "My mom is on her way," she replied.

The nurse disappeared again before Becca could ask her any other questions.

Sighing with terror, Becca looked around trying to keep tears at bay. When she spotted her mother and Ben sprinting across the well-lit entrance, she lost her composure.

"How is he, Becca?" Lydia asked her, enveloping her daughter in a protective hug.

"I don't know. They went to check, then asked if I was here alone. I told them you were on the way," she explained halfheartedly.

They sat down together and Ben leaned into them, "Do you know what happened?" he asked cautiously.

Becca wiped at the tears that just kept coming now, "The officer said there was an accident, that's all. With another car," she shook her head and shrugged.

Ben reached over and gripped Becca's hand, giving her a sympathetic smile.

Not long after his grip tightened, they saw a doctor walking toward them.

"Mrs. Enders?"

Becca's head snapped at his voice and she got to her feet, "Yes, where is Jamie?"

"I'm Dr. Myers," he paused and cleared his throat, "do you know what happened to your husband, Mrs. Enders?"

"An accident," she answered. She squeezed her eyes shut. Deep down in the pit of her soul she knew why no one would answer her question.

"An impaired driver veered into Mr. Enders' lane of traffic," he paused again, taking his glasses off and slipping them into a pocket, "he struck your husbands vehicle in the driver's side door. Your husband skidded and hit an electric power pole on the left side. The other driver sustained minor injuries and is being questioned."

Becca glared at the doctor, but couldn't form words.

"Doctor," Lydia asked sternly, "Jamie. How is Jamie?"

Becca gulped in air and held her breath. Everything seemed to be in slow motion. She watched as the doctor shook his head solemnly. It sounded as if she were in a silent tunnel when he told them Jamie had suffered many injuries and despite their best efforts, didn't make it. He apologized sincerely and walked away.

Becca stood still. She could feel numbness take over her body. In her mind, every memory of Jamie played like a fast forwarding movie. She wanted to reach out and touch those memories.

She felt Lydia wrap her arms around her as she collapsed into the chair. She sat in shock for an eternity, her eyes darting, her brain buzzing.

When she looked at her mother's sad, tear stained face, the volume of the room rushed back to Becca's ears and it was all so suddenly apparent.

Becca leaned over and buried her head in her mother's embrace and sobbed for hours.

When she was physically exhausted and drained of tears, they left.

The sun was breaching the horizon as they drove home. Ben riding with Becca, Lydia following them.

Becca was alternating between complete numbness and unsatisfying aching as she drove. She'd sob and stop and then repeat. She wondered why no one asked if she'd like to see Jamie one last time. She wondered why she didn't ask to. She wondered how she'd continue to breathe from one minute to the next. She wondered if she actually cared.

Reaching their house, Becca fought to climb the stairs. She wanted to be in bed, in their bed, but it made her sick to think Jamie would never be back in that bed.

Her mother and Ben settled in the living room, quietly talking.

Finally, in their bedroom, Becca closed the door behind her. She kicked off her shoes and stripped off her clothes. The clothes she had been wearing to go away with Jamie. She let them fall and grabbed the first thing she saw, her night shirt from the night before. She tugged it on and moved around the room, closing blinds and pulling the curtains tight. It was as dark as possible. She stood staring at the bed. Flashes of memories of the past twelve years flooded her mind. High school. College. Colorado. Buying the house. Christmases. His smile. His laughter. Their wedding. Their discussions on starting their family. Their love.

In the midst of the overflow of sadness in the one comforting thought was their love. Becca and Jamie loved each other with everything that they had. With their entire selves. There was certainly no two other people who could feel as strongly about each other as they did. Every day they loved each other. Every day Becca felt lucky to have him in her life. To have him as her life.

And now that was gone.

He was gone.

Her life was gone.

Their love was gone.

Becca clenched her teeth and ran to her bathroom, becoming physically ill. When her body expelled all it had except for shudders and tears, she folded back the covers on their bed and slipped in, laying down where Jamie would normally be sleeping. She tried shaking all thoughts from her head.

She rolled to her stomach, buried her face into the pillow that still smelled like Jamie and screamed. Loudly, she screamed, from the deepest of places in her soul, she screamed until she was breathless and her head throbbed.

Then she cried.